How to
Interview
Sexual
Abuse
Victims

Interpersonal Violence:
The Practice Series
Jon R. Conte, Series Editor

Interpersonal Violence: The Practice Series is devoted to mental health, social service, and allied professionals who confront daily the problem of interpersonal violence. It is hoped that the knowledge, professional experience, and high standards of practice offered by the authors of these volumes may lead to the end of interpersonal violence.

In this series...

How to
Interview
Sexual
Abuse
Victims

Including the Use
of Anatomical Dolls

Marcia Morgan

With Contributions From
Virginia Edwards

Interpersonal Violence:
The Practice Series

SAGE Publications
International Educational and Professional Publisher
Thousand Oaks   London   New Delhi

For information address:

SAGE Publications, Inc.
2455 Teller Road
Thousand Oaks, California 91320

SAGE Publications Ltd.
6 Bonhill Street
London EC2A 4PU
United Kingdom

SAGE Publications India Pvt. Ltd.
M-32 Market
Greater Kailash I
New Delhi 110048 India

Printed in the United States of America

Library of Congress Cataloging-in-Publication Data

Morgan, Marcia K.
    How to interview sexual abuse victims : including the use of
  anatomical dolls/Marcia Morgan with contributions from Virginia
Edwards.
        p. cm.—(Interpersonal violence : The practice series; v. 7)
    Includes bibliographical references and index.
    ISBN 0-8039-5288-0.—ISBN 0-8039-5289-9 (pbk.)
    1. Child sexual abuse—Investigation. 2. Interviewing in child
abuse. I. Edwards, Virginia, 1947-   . II. Title. III. Series.
HV8079.C48M67   1994
363.2'59536—dc20   94-29569
                                                             CIP

95 96 97 98 99 10 9 8 7 6 5 4 3 2

Sage Production Editor: Gillian Dickens

This book is dedicated to my
father, Les Morgan, whose love,
creativity, encouragement, and
support will always be in my
heart and in my life.

A special thank you to Joelle Steward for her research assistance on this project and to Virginia "Ginger" Edwards for sharing her expertise in working with young children. Without joining forces, Ginger and I would have never developed the anatomical dolls . . . and this book would have never become a reality.

Contents

Declaration

This book is intended to provide an introduction and a broad set of guidelines on how to interview children about sexual abuse. Individual practice with children may vary from that outlined here and still be competent and professional.

Introduction

Sexual abuse of children is not an easy thing to talk about—it has long been ignored by society. Yet it must be discussed. Every day in the news there are reports of children being sexually abused in day care centers, by relatives, in homes, in social clubs, and even by older children. It is estimated that approximately one out of every four girls and one out of every eight boys will be a victim of sexual abuse by the time he or she reaches his or her 18th birthday.

Child sexual abuse, whether fondling or forcible intercourse, is a safety issue of importance to the entire community. Abused children often reach adulthood with unresolved conflicts, extreme insecurity, and a confused attitude toward authority. Their uncertainty, anger, and hatred may be turned against themselves, their friends, their own children, and society. A vast number of criminals convicted of robbery, burglary, rape, and arson were physically or sexually abused and/or neglected as children. Convicted male felons are five times more likely to have been abused than noninstitutionalized males. Likewise, national studies reveal that on the average, 80% of incarcerated felons were physically or sexually abused as children. One of the most alarming facts is that sexually abused children are more likely to grow up to be child abusers themselves—and the cycle of abuse continues.

This book is designed for professional interviewers, including police, social service workers, and prosecutors. The purpose is to provide interviewing guidelines that not only will enhance the amount, quality, and validity of information obtained from a child, but will create an environment that minimizes the child's trauma. The book begins by describing how the criminal justice system has dealt with child victims and how the anatomical dolls were created as an interviewing tool. It examines the problems professionals face with young children and how preinterview preparation is essential for a successful interview. The book walks the reader through an interview from beginning to end: establishing rapport, avoiding leading questions, deciding whether to use anatomical dolls, how to use dolls appropriately, case law and legal issues, and going to trial. Additionally, the book includes training exercises, a glossary of terms, an annotated bibliography, and a listing of audiovisual resources.

Much has been written about interviewing children. This book, however, is designed to provide the professional with basic ideas on interviewing of children that incorporates current case law and practice on the use of anatomical dolls. The in-depth discussion is based not only on the many years' experience of the author, who was the cocreator of the dolls, but on current research as well. The book is a comprehensive look at the very complex task of interviewing children. Although there is a great deal condensed in the following pages, the reader may also find other materials outlined in the appendices helpful.

1

Children and Anatomical Dolls

❏ History of Child Crime Victims

Historically, children have always been victims of abuse. These acts were often tolerated or even encouraged because of society's view of children's rights. New norms and expectations developed as childhood became a special phase in the life cycle. Yet adults seemed much more concerned about children committing crimes and deviating from the norms than about children being recipients of crime.

The creation of laws applicable to children in the 19th century and of the American juvenile court system in Illinois in 1899 emerged as a way to control children in a pseudo-parental role. Because children were now viewed as different from adults, special laws and a separate legal system were consistent with this changing attitude.

So too was the unique way in which this culture eventually became concerned about child victims. The American Humane Society, an organization for the prevention of cruelty to animals, was established in the United States around the early part of the century. It eventually

1

began keeping statistics on child abuse victimization rates, and continued up until 1985.

During the 1970s and 1980s, there was increased media attention on child physical and sexual victimization, with federal monies set aside to confront this problem. Special procedures and protocols were established in all 50 states to accommodate young victims. They included training social workers, police, hospital staff, attorneys, and judges regarding sensitivity in evaluations, assessments, investigation, and treatment of child victims. Special preparation for the courtroom and trial, Guardian Ad Litum programs, videotaping a child's testimony rather than having the child come face-to-face with the defendant in the courtroom, and sensitivity in interviews and cross-examination were all encouraged to ensure swift and accurate prosecution with minimal emotional damage to the child. Yet problems surfaced, frequently at the first adult-child interaction when the crime was reported or revealed. The communication problems between the adult and child had to be addressed in order for the case to be able to proceed in the criminal justice system or juvenile court. One way to bridge the communication gap was using anatomical dolls and having them be an accepted interviewing tool in the criminal justice, social service, and mental health community.

❑ History of Dolls

Archeological records reveal that children in prehistoric times enjoyed playing with dolls just as much as children do today. Dolls made of wood, clay, and bones have been found in the ancient graves of children in every part of the world.

Explorers of cliff dwellings in the southwestern part of the United States found dolls made of cottonwood sticks wrapped with skirts made of cedar bark and cotton rags. Collectors have found colonial dolls made with stuffed cloth bodies, prim painted faces, tiny pointed feet, and old-fashioned clothes. They have also found dolls made of animal skins stuffed with sawdust or cork and heads made of wax, papier-mâché, and even china.

Egyptian dolls dating back to about 2000 B.C. were called paddle dolls because they were carved from flat pieces of wood shaped like paddles. They were painted with patterns to look like clothes and had strings of clay beads to represent hair. Paddle dolls were religious figures and were buried with the dead to provide them with servants in the next world.

> *Yet dolls were not always toys.*

Doll-like figures from Greek and Roman tombs dating from about 300 B.C. had jointed, movable arms and legs. Some were carved from bone or ivory, but most were made of clay or wood. Scholars have not determined whether these were toys or religious objects.

In the Middle Ages, dolls were viewed as dangerous instruments for children, used only by magicians and witches. In Napoleon's day, miniatures such as dolls and houses were accepted as enjoyment for adults and children alike. In 1600, during the time of Louis XIII, boys and girls (and Louis himself) played with dolls.

Yet dolls were not always toys. In early French history, fashion dolls were sent to other countries to show the latest in Paris fashion trends. During the Victorian era, in order to spare embarrassment and to maintain modesty, women used a doll to help explain their physical ailments to a doctor. In the 1970s, anatomical dolls appeared in the social services/criminal justice system as a communication tool for young male and female sexual abuse victims.

❑ **What Is an Anatomical Doll?**

Anatomical dolls are soft, cloth dolls that are a general replica of the human body, complete with sexual body parts such as a penis and testicles for male dolls, vaginal opening for female dolls, oral and anal openings, and pubic hair on the adults. The dolls are sometimes referred to as "anatomically complete" or "anatomically correct," which is not completely accurate because they do not have *all* body parts. The dolls were designed simply to be a basic representation or map of the human body. Using anatomical dolls, a child can demonstrate any form of sexual abuse (e.g., rape, sodomy) that may have occurred. This helps to minimize the communication problem inherent in talking with children about sexual issues and can also reduce the trauma for the child.

❏ How Anatomical Dolls Were Created

The use of anatomical dolls for interviews with abused children began in 1976 in Eugene, Oregon. Virginia Friedemann Edwards, Marcia Morgan, and Mike Whitney, then working on a special interagency rape team project with the Springfield police, the Lane County sheriff's office, and the Eugene police, respectively, created the dolls out of a need for better communication with children. Morgan bought the original set of two adult dolls from a local seamstress. Later, they redesigned the dolls, based on their experience in using them in legal interviews, trials, and classroom prevention presentations. They made them less toylike and more sexually explicit by adding oral, anal, and vaginal body openings; neutral facial expressions so that the child could communicate a full range of emotions; three skin colors; and both child and adult models. Although stuffed animals and ordinary plastic dolls had long been used by counselors in play therapy, this was the first time an anatomical doll had been used as an aid in the investigation of child sexual abuse.

In 1980, Edwards, Morgan, and Whitney formed a business, Migima Designs (the name created out of the first two initials of their three first names), in order to make the dolls, develop prevention, treatment, and investigation educational materials, and provide professional training and consulting to others in the field. Their dolls began receiving national attention in 1981 with an appearance on *The Phil Donahue Show*. Since that time, their dolls and books, videos, cassette tapes, lectures, consultations, expert testimony, and training seminars have been featured on *Good Morning America, 60 Minutes*; in *Redbook, Glamour,* and *Reader's Digest* magazines; and in numerous newspapers throughout the country. Several other doll manufacturing companies have been formed since that time. The dolls and educational materials are being used in all 50 states, all Canadian provinces, and over 30 foreign countries.

❏ How to Select Anatomical Dolls

There are many different types of anatomical dolls; some are professionally made, some are homemade. In either case, it is important to choose your dolls carefully. Factors such as size, appearance, and material can play a major role in determining whether the dolls are effective in facilitating communication about suspected sexual abuse. Using special anatomical dolls rather than the child's own doll could prevent negative feelings from becoming associated with a loved toy.

The physical appearance and structure of the dolls can also make or break a case. A defense attorney could claim that the dolls' sexual parts were disproportionate, or that the facial expressions were such that they "led" the interviews or were suggestive.

You will need a minimum of four dolls: a male adult, a female adult, a male child, and a female child. However, it is generally recommended to have six or eight dolls, including a female grandparent, a male grandparent, and an additional adult female and adult male to represent other extended family and other people involved in the case. More than two to four dolls may overwhelm some children. Keep extra dolls available but out of sight and use if needed. If you work with children of different races, it is helpful to have sets of dolls in the appropriate skin tones. This means you may need a total of eight to 12 dolls.

Listed below are some guidelines for use that will help you select anatomical dolls appropriate for use when interviewing children.

SIZE OF DOLLS

Ideally, the length should be approximately 20 in. for adult dolls and 16 in. for child dolls. The waist of the dolls should not exceed 8 in. This is a comfortable size for most children to hold and maneuver.

Larger dolls are much more difficult to manipulate, and children may get frustrated trying to demonstrate what happened. If the dolls are much smaller, it may be difficult for the interviewer, judge, or jury to see what the child is doing with the dolls.

OPENINGS

All dolls should have oral and anal openings. Both the adult and child female dolls should also have vaginal openings. The penis should be able to fit easily into any of these openings. Some dolls come with tongues, which may be helpful in establishing specific details in cases involving oral sex. Some defense attorneys may state that the very nature of a doll having body orifices is leading the child in the interview (see Chapter 7). There has been less concern about this matter when the inner pockets of the orifices are the same color as the skin.

SEXUAL BODY PARTS

The penis and testicles should be proportionate to the rest of the body and in the correct location. If one is purchasing "homemade" dolls, this can be an issue. If the penis is too large, for instance, it may be viewed as suggestive or leading the child. In other words, the sexual parts might "direct" the child to think about sexual things that he or she wouldn't have noticed or thought about. However, a study exploring the issue of proportionality by measuring breasts and genitalia of 17 sets of anatomical dolls found that when the measurements were extrapolated to adult human proportions, the sizes of the genitalia and breasts were not in fact exaggerated (Bays, 1990; see Chapter 11). Be prepared, however, for the defense attorney to raise the issue of sexual suggestiveness. Purchasing commercially made dolls that have been "tested" in court may prevent this problem.

The penis and testicles should be proportionate to the rest of the body.

Additionally, some dolls come with circumcised and noncircumcised penises. Although this may be more detail than you need in establishing the details of the case, it is an option to consider when selecting dolls. Sometimes these penises are held on with velcro and are detachable, or may come with an erect or flaccid penis attached by velcro. In either case, the child may take this body part on and off at will.

The merits of the detachable penis are debated by professionals in the field. Many feel that in an interview conducted by a child protective service worker or police officer, this distraction can be more distressing than helpful. The notion of ripping off genitals, complete with the noise associated with the velcro, is violent and not "anatomically correct." Boys might find it particularly concerning to think their penis can be pulled off. Where the detachable penis may be useful is when the dolls are used in ongoing therapy and in the context of an expression of anger or communication.

The breasts and vagina should also be proportionate, or the dolls may be viewed as sexually suggestive and directing the child's thinking and behavior. The vagina should not be in the front of the doll but rather lower, between the legs. It should be of significant size so that the penis can fit into it easily. Some female dolls now have a clitoris, which could be useful if digital or oral manipulation was part of the sexual abuse.

BODY

The dolls' bodies should be soft to the touch so that they are comforting for the child. Because the dolls often get thrown, hit, and abused, they should be made of a nonbreakable material.

SKIN TONE

The dolls' skin tone should reflect the racial make-up of your clients and community. Children will find it easier to relate to dolls that look like themselves. If you work with children from many different racial backgrounds, consider obtaining dolls with skin tones of white (Caucasian), light brown (appropriate for Hispanic, Asian, and Native American populations), and dark brown (appropriate for African American populations).

SAFETY

The dolls should be made of nontoxic, nonflammable materials. The faces should not have buttons for eyes or other features a child could pull off and swallow. Wires inside a doll to hold the body in position can be dangerous because they may poke through the doll's skin.

The stuffing in the dolls should be nonallergenic, such as a polyester fiberfill.

FACE AND HAIR

The face should be pleasant but not "cutesy" or clownlike. The doll's hair should be realistic in color and not too bright. Jurors want to know that the child is telling the truth about an incident with the dolls, not "playing" or making up a story with the dolls.

The expression on all the dolls' faces should be neutral to allow the children to demonstrate a variety of emotions (fear, confusion, happiness, etc.). Additionally, the neutral expression is essential if the dolls are used in court. If there is a slight deviation from one doll's face to the next, the interview may be questioned. For example, the interview could be challenged because the adult male doll, unlike the other dolls, had eyebrows that were tilted inward and a mouth slightly turned downward at the corners. The defense attorney might state that the adult male looked "sinister" and therefore was suggestive to the child. To ensure consistency of facial expressions, try to select dolls with silk-screened or machine-embroidered faces rather than hand-painted faces.

WASHABLE

The dolls should be durable and completely washable. It is generally best to hand wash or machine wash on gentle and in cold water. Partially tumble dry or line dry them. The dolls will probably get a lot of use, so be sure they are kept clean.

2

Problems in Interviewing Sexual Abuse Victims

Interviewing children who have been sexually abused is not an easy task. If we recognize and anticipate the basic communication problems that may arise, we are better able to apply effective interviewing strategies to alleviate these roadblocks. Many children are reluctant to talk about sexual abuse, regardless of whether the interviewer is a police officer, social worker, counselor, or doctor. This reluctance stems from four major factors: fear, a limited vocabulary, embarrassment, and developmental level.

❑ Fear

The child victim may simply fear talking to an adult, especially a stranger. The child may be afraid of not being listened to or believed. Because of your size, age, race, or sex, you may unknowingly resemble the offender. The child may know you are a "cop" or someone "official" and may fear getting into trouble. This is why "doing your homework" before the interview is important. Fear, whether real or perceived, can be all-encompassing to a child. It is important that you as an interviewer acknowledge this fear and try to work with it.

Fear may take many forms and is one of the biggest roadblocks to communication. Often the offender has told the child that if he or she ever "tells" anyone about what happened, the offender will get in trouble and be sent to jail. The child may feel that discussing the abuse would be breaking a promise or a vow of secrecy. On one hand, the child may fear the threats made by the offender. At the same time, the child may fear the discontinuation of affection and attention by the offender and feel the need to protect this person. In many cases, disclosing the event is an emotional dilemma for the child, who may believe it is better to have some attention from the offender, even if it is scary or confusing, than to have no attention or "love" at all.

❏ Vocabulary

Communication with the child is critical because the existence of a crime and the nature of the crime cannot be established without specific details. However, most children do not have a vocabulary sophisticated enough to discuss a sexual abuse. The child you are interviewing may not know the correct names for parts of the body and may need to rely on "baby talk." It can be confusing for the interviewer when the child calls a vagina a "poo-poo" or a "front bottom." It may be embarrassing if the child relies on slang or street language, calling a vagina a "pussy" or a penis a "cock." It is very difficult when the child does not understand the terminology the interviewer uses and the interviewer does not understand what the child is trying to say. This difficulty is compounded when a non-English-speaking or mentally handicapped victim is involved.

Many children may simply not know how to tell someone about the abuse. A child may say, "Mr. O'Brien wears funny-looking underpants" or "I don't like to play at Susie's house anymore." If an interviewer is able to delve into these two statements more thoroughly, it may become apparent that Mr. O'Brien was taking off his pants in front of the child and masturbating, or that Susie has been fondling the child. Or it could mean the child simply saw Mr. O'Brien's underpants folded on the dryer and they had funny little hearts or designs on them.

In either case, try to establish a common language base between yourself and the child and pursue statements that may be hiding relevant facts. Specific interviewing techniques will be discussed later in the book.

❑ Embarrassment

Generally speaking, sexual issues are not openly discussed in our society. Children learn very young not to masturbate in the grocery store, tell jokes about bodily functions, play "doctor" with their friends, or run around the neighborhood nude. It is hard for most children to switch gears and realize that you, the interviewer, have given them permission to talk about something sexual. It may also be embarrassing and too personal for the child to point to the sexual parts of his or her own body to describe what happened, or to indicate where the touching occurred. Sexual abuse victims are often self-conscious about their bodies and think they somehow "look different" because of their experience.

Children who have been abused are also concerned about what other kids will say if they find out about the abuse. Friends and siblings can be cruel to one another, embarrassing each other with name calling or labeling. Victims who are sexually abused by a person of the same sex may fear the embarrassment of being labeled a homosexual. Even the thought of peer reactions can be a tremendous roadblock to effective communication.

Learn to recognize and appreciate these feelings. The use of anatomical dolls is often an aid in breaking through the barrier of self-consciousness and embarrassment because the child can point to and talk about the sexual act by using the doll as a neutral, third-party object.

❑ Developmental Level

Parents and teachers can verify that many children have short attention spans. Young children can be especially restless and difficult to keep on one topic for any length of time. This is particularly true if the interview is quite long. Dolls make an interview interesting, thus holding the child's attention. They often help the interviewer complete the session more quickly and effectively.

Age and/or developmental level may also be a problem when trying to establish a child's credibility in court. Defense attorneys often argue that a young child can be easily persuaded or led in an interview. Children are told to obey adults, and unless your words are chosen carefully and dolls used appropriately, the attorney may accuse you of persuading the child to disclose something sexual. As a result, valuable information obtained in an interview may be challenged in court. Keep in mind that the younger the victim, the more likely you are to be challenged on your interviewing techniques. Therefore it is important to have a good understanding of child development—what children understand, how they construct and view their world, and how they might interpret your questions. This can best be gained by reading books, by taking classes, and by learning through experience. Chapter 3 will discuss in more detail children's cognitive abilities as these relate to gathering information in an interview.

3

Preinterview Preparation

To conduct a good interview with a victim of child sexual abuse, you need to be very well-prepared. Rarely are there witnesses to child sexual abuse, and medical evidence is often hard to obtain. Even when the medical evidence does exist, it is seldom more than support for the child's story. This means that legal action against an offender generally relies on the victim's clear and unequivocal information about the abusive incident or series of incidents. If you are unable to help the child victim provide this information, the offender may remain free to abuse again.

Preinterview preparation begins by gathering adequate background information. Knowing something about the child and his or her family may help you create an environment in which the child will share what has happened and ask questions in a way the child will understand. The more you know about the child, the more prepared you will be in selecting the most effective and appropriate "interview tools." Sometimes you will be working as a team with other professionals. Interviewing as a team is different from interviewing by yourself, and therefore requires additional types of preinterview preparation. And finally, choosing the appropriate location for conducting the interview can have a tremendous impact on whether your interview is successful. Each of these factors needs to be addressed prior to an interview with a child sexual abuse victim. To help you do this effectively, each of these preparation steps is discussed in more detail.

❏ Gathering Background Information

A variety of background information is useful to you during an interview with a child who may have been sexually abused. Some of this information should be gathered before the interview takes place and will help you to conduct an interview that is both sensitive and productive. Your goal is to create an environment in which the child feels free to talk to you, even about very personal matters. Because you are probably a stranger, this may not be easy to do. Talking about personal matters, and especially sexual matters, with a stranger is not only difficult but generally considered inappropriate in our society. It's important to remember that you are asking a child to share something that is very intimate and, at the same time, to go against his or her perception of what is socially correct. In addition, the child may have been specifically told not to talk about these activities. Gathering sufficient background information can often help make the interview easier for the child and for you.

One source of background information available to you is provided in previous reports concerning the child or the child's family. Check your own agency's files for any previous contacts made with the child or with members of the child's family. In order to seek additional information, contact the appropriate police department or child protective service agency with whom you work.

The following are the types of questions that an interviewer may want to ask regarding the child's background information. This will help give you a picture of the child's world, key people in his or her life, and issues of importance to the child.

- What information do the agencies have on file?
- Are there any previous reports of abuse?
- Is there any history of mental disability?
- Does any member of the family have a criminal record?
- Has the family's pattern of interaction ever raised the concern of school personnel or any welfare organization?
- With whom is the child currently living?
- How long has this been the case?

Another source of background information is the current report of suspected abuse. Carefully review the information obtained when the report was made and find out who wrote the report because he or she may bring into this information his or her own perspective and bias. For example, was the report made by a neighbor who has been feuding with the offender over unrelated issues? Was the report made by a parent who is divorcing the alleged offender? Is the officer who wrote the report known for strongly disliking working sexual abuse cases and believing that most are "made up" anyway? Is there any relationship, past or present, with the report writer and any parties involved in this case? Any of these scenarios could bring into question issues of bias in the report. Other general questions to ask include:

- How old is the child?
- What sex is the child?
- Did the child report a specific incident of abuse to someone?
- If so, to whom did the child report it?
- Was the report made as a result of someone's observation or following an accidental disclosure?
- How much information is already known about the suspected abuse?
- Has a specific offender been identified?
- If so, is this person someone with whom the child lives?
- Have there been other reports of sexual abuse in the neighborhood?
- Where is the child now?
- If at school, how long will the child be there before classes are dismissed?

Whenever possible, interview the person who first reported the suspected abuse. This person may be able to provide you with useful information about the child and serve as a link between you and the child. Because you will probably be able to gather more information by making personal contact, it is best if you can talk to this person face-to-face, not over the telephone. The person who made the report is often more open when you meet personally, and you have the additional advantage of being able to observe gestures and emotions. Some questions that you might ask are:

- Did the child talk directly to this person about the reported sexual abuse?
- If not, what was it that made this person suspect sexual abuse had occurred?
- What, specifically, does this person know about the abuse?
- What were the exact words the child used?
- Can this person tell you anything about the child's personality?
- Does he or she know anything about the child's interests or hobbies?
- What can this person tell you about the child's family or the suspected abuser?
- Is this person willing to introduce you to the child?

Gathering psychosocial information from family members may be useful as well. This might include finding out about family attitudes and behaviors toward nudity, sexuality, privacy, availability of sexually explicit materials including access to cable television, mental history of the caregiver, divorce, and custody and visitation issues. Parents and guardians should be directed not to discuss the incident with the child until after the interview.

Collecting background information takes time. It also takes good interpersonal skills and a sensitivity to the concerns and insecurities of other people. The effort is worth it, however. When you interview the child sexual abuse victim you may have only one opportunity to create an environment in which the child can talk freely and comfortably. The more information you have, the greater your chances of achieving this goal. Knowledge of a child's interests and hobbies, for example, can be used at the beginning of an interview to establish rapport. Furthermore, knowing how and why a report was initiated will help you predict what will be needed in the interview and help you to establish the necessary level of comfort. For example, a child making a direct report may be seeking help and may be more open to assistance from others. However, a child who is approached for an interview after a vague or accidental disclosure may be confused or afraid to talk further. A willingness to gather necessary background information is the sign of a dedicated professional, and will always result in a better interview.

It should be noted that the idea of gathering information about the alleged sexual abuse from others prior to interviewing the child is controversial. Some practitioners and researchers, such as Dr. Sue White in Cleveland, Ohio, have proposed that this practice has the potential to contaminate the objectivity of the interviewer and in turn the interview. "Blind interviews" only give the interviewer the first name and age of the child. Background information or specifics about the alleged abuse from the reporting party are not disclosed beforehand. Therefore the interviewer does not have a hidden motivation, a subliminal agenda, or the appearance of one.

As discussed in the research literature, by withholding information about a suspected abuser, what he or she allegedly did, the child's history, or other allegations, potential sources of bias are removed. Blind interviews are generally more openly received by the legal system and eventually may be mandatory. The issue of the interviewer's coercion, suggestion, and leading questions is minimized.

Blind interviews require interviewers to rely heavily on rapport developed with the child, knowledge of child development, and general interview skills. Yet they place the interviewer in a position of having to "start from scratch" when talking to a child. This may take a great deal of time and require the child to be attentive for a long period. Therefore with very young children with short attention spans, blind interviews may not work as well.

Many professionals are trying to reach a balance in the type of information they receive prior to the interview. Basic information is needed but should be limited and standardized so as not to bias or appear to bias the interview.

Figure 3.1. A Variety of Interviewing Tools

❏ Selecting Interview Tools

When talking with children, it is helpful to gather together a variety of emotionally expressive toys and items to be used in the interviewing process. Each child will have a different attention span and a different way in which he or she will communicate. Being prepared and flexible to respond to the child's communication needs is essential. Store the following items in a convenient, easily accessible place when interviewing a child:

- blank paper
- coloring books (not specific to sexual abuse)
- crayons

- modeling clay or play dough
- toy telephone
- hand puppets
- stuffed animals
- anatomical drawings
- anatomical dolls
- doll house

Supplies such as paper, crayons, coloring books, and clay are excellent rapport builders for children of many different ages. By doing something familiar, children will usually relax and conversation will flow more easily. For very young children, the coloring or drawing will provide some release for their nervous energy. Blank paper and crayons can also be useful later in the interview if a child wants to draw or demonstrate something that has happened in the past or the abuse itself. A toy telephone can be useful when trying to make contact with a very shy child. In addition, a toy telephone may be a way for a child to reveal embarrassing details without having to say them to someone face-to-face.

Anatomical or regular hand puppets can be another effective way to engage children and are also useful in helping children to talk about things that are hard to share. In this way, they can help to depersonalize an interview by allowing a child to project any abuse that has occurred onto a puppet. Although generally not used when establishing rapport, the anatomical dolls can be extremely useful during the actual interview to help children explain and describe any incidents of sexual abuse (more on this in the next chapter).

Being well-prepared with a variety of toys and visual items will give you maximum flexibility in responding to each child's unique communication styles. Be aware, however, that having too many of these tools out at once during the interview could be distracting.

❏ Interviewing as a Team

There are advantages in interviewing a child as part of a team. The most common interviewing team consists of two professionals, one representing the legal profession and one representing the social service profession. By interviewing as a team, it is often possible to gather a more complete picture of what has happened. The team approach can also give a child more people in his or her support system. This can be very helpful, especially if there is a prolonged investigation and lengthy legal proceedings. Before a team interview, it is important for both professionals to review the information that has been gathered and to discuss a manner for working together during the interview. The team may believe it is best to have one person do the interview and the other observe out of sight, such as through a one-way mirror. Decisions should be made as to how to start the interview and who the lead interviewer will be. It is also important that both professionals acknowledge the need to be sensitive to the child and to the child's situation.

Children react to team interviews in varying ways. It is useful if you and your interviewing partner can discuss strategies for accommodating the child's specific needs. For example, you may find that two people taking notes is very distracting to the child being interviewed. This problem can be resolved easily: One interviewer can do most of the talking, while the other takes notes to be shared later. In some interviews, the child needs considerable support in order to share what has happened. When interviewing as a team, one interviewer can act as a support person (assisting and encouraging the child), while the other asks the necessary questions. Sometimes a child will indicate a desire to be interviewed by only one of the members of an interviewing team, and this preference should be respected. Occasionally, an interviewer may physically remind the child of the offender (e.g., the interviewer's beard, mannerisms, clothing), causing the child to be reluctant to talk. It is also common for children to be able to communicate with people of one sex better than another. For this reason, it may be helpful if the interviewing team is made up of one male and one female.

Using the team approach for interviewing has many benefits. It is often possible to elicit more information from the child victim and therefore build a stronger investigative case. In addition, team interviews will result in two sets of observations and two sets of insights into the case. It is common for one member of a team to pick up on something the other member failed to notice. The team approach can also result in more support to the child and to the child's family, thus increasing the chances that future intervention will be seen as something positive and helpful. The quality of the initial contact with a victim of child sexual abuse often determines the family's ability to recognize and accept help from the entire system in the months ahead. Your skill as a team can be a major factor in starting this process in a positive and healing manner.

❏ Choosing a Location

One of the most important decisions prior to the interview is choosing a location. The location in which an interview is conducted will greatly influence whether a child talks openly to you. Good locations for interviewing children who may have been sexually abused at home include the home of the person who reported the abuse, the home of a family friend, or the child's school or day care center. Although an office at the police department or child protective services agency may provide privacy, these are not generally good locations for an initial interview. Until a caseworker or police officer becomes a trusted person, such offices may be scary places to a child. Many communities, however, now offer a safe interview room located at a child advocacy or assessment center. Such a setting offers a less official atmosphere with child-size furniture, a comfortable floor, and pleasant colors (such as soft pastels) and decorations that are not too stimulating and distracting.

Generally, the least desirable location for an interview is the family home. This is primarily due to the extreme difficulty in having much control over this environment. Parents, even those who are supportive of their child's disclosure, may be hesitant to allow a private interview or may disrupt one after it has started. Family members will sometimes physically prevent you from seeing a child or try to dissuade a child from talking with you. The child's home may also be the place where abusive incidents occurred and consequently not a place where the child feels safe. This may raise a child's anxiety and thus contribute to or inhibit disclosure. You will need to assess this yourself. If it appears truly to hinder disclosure, ask the child if he or she would be more comfortable talking somewhere else. If this location is not clearly identified as a barrier to communication, do not assume it is the problem. Note, however, that with very young children, it may be helpful to interview them at the scene of the abuse to trigger memory.

If it becomes necessary to interview a child in his or her home, the following guidelines will help to make the interview more productive:

1. Approach the child at a time when the suspected abuser is not at home.
2. Do your best to insist on privacy. This means an interview with no other family members present and a room with a door that can be closed.
3. Do not use the child's bedroom unless he or she prefers to meet in that room. Because a large majority of abusive incidents occur in the child's own room, being there could heighten the child's anxiety.
4. Try to find a location outside the house: for example, a private spot in the backyard or in your car. Never choose a spot where you might be interrupted by a telephone call or pager during an interview.

When looking for a location in which to conduct the interview, remember that your goal is to provide a safe, private setting where you can talk to the child without interruptions. The site that you choose should provide both visual and auditory privacy. Distracting sights and sounds will always result in a longer interview than necessary and, for very young children, may make the task of staying on one topic virtually impossible. Children will also be more reluctant to talk if they feel someone else may be watching or listening. This level of privacy is equally important when conducting an interview at the child's school or some other location outside the home. Friends or siblings may assume a child talking to a stranger is in trouble and may alert the child's family. If parents or other relatives arrive at the interview location before you have finished, their presence usually means the end of an effective interview.

❏ Getting Started

Once you have gathered available background information, selected your interviewing tools, discussed procedure with your team member, and chosen a possible interview location, you are ready to get started. Always try to allow yourself sufficient time for an interview with a child. It is important that neither you nor the child feel pressured to hurry the interview. Some of the factors that frequently contribute to "hurrying" through an interview include the school bus schedule, time for lunch break, the child needing to

> *Allow yourself sufficient time for an interview with a child.*

use the bathroom, nap time, or an approaching end to the workday. Avoid letting these factors influence the manner in which you conduct an interview. A sense of urgency on your part may give the child a strong message that he or she is less important to you than these other matters. It is also possible that the child will attempt to wait you out, concluding that continued silence will result in an early end to the interview.

When you arrive at the interview site, it is important that you talk to the other adults who are there, especially those who can assist you in conducting an effective interview (e.g., the child's principal or teacher, the nonabusive parent, relatives). Advise them that you will need a private time with the child in order to conduct your investigation. If there are concerns about whether any abuse actually occurred, let them know that it is just as important to establish that there isn't a problem as to confirm that there is. Indicate that you will need an unlimited amount of time with the child and that there should be no interruptions, for any reason. Try to explain that it is important for the child not to be pressured during the interview and that the child needs to feel free to talk openly, without being "on guard." If you are using an office that belongs to someone else, suggest this person remove any papers that may be needed and arrange for phone calls to be taken elsewhere. Likewise, be sure that if you have a beeper or are carrying a cellular phone, it is turned off during an interview and out of view of the child.

Show the adults your interviewing tools, including the anatomical dolls. Briefly explain how you intend to use these tools. This information will help to assure them that you will be talking to the child in a sensitive and professional manner. Indicate that what the child tells you will have to remain confidential, at least for the time being. Try to explain that children who have been abused often think they have done something wrong and therefore parents (who believe their child and are not involved in the abuse) and other significant adults can play an important role as support persons. The child should also be allowed to decide if and when details of the abuse are to be shared with them. Help the adults present at the interview site to understand the need for privacy and to respect it. You may also want to give them names of local support groups for parents of abused children.

When you are ready to meet with the child, ask one of the trusted adults to introduce you. Let this person know that the child will feel more comfortable if you are introduced as someone who can be helpful. For example, you might suggest that the person say, "This is Ms. Watson. She works for Child Protective Services. Part of her job is talking to children, and I'm sure she will listen to anything you want to tell her." Another possibility might be: "Officer Brown is here to talk with you. I called him because I know he talks to lots of children. He has helped me a lot when I have questions or problems."

Be prepared for resistance or temper tantrums prior to or during an interview. It is not unusual for children to be afraid and reluctant to go with you. Calmly but firmly state, "We need to go to my room" or "We need to talk—let's go to my room where you and I are going to talk." Do not give the child an out by saying, "OK?" or asking, "Will you come to my room?" If the child says "no," the communication gap widens and the power struggle escalates.

In summary, there are a number of things to do before you approach a child for an initial interview. Background checks, gathering tools, and reviewing information with your team member can all take time. In addition, talking to the person who made the report and choosing an interview location may further delay your response to a report of suspected sexual abuse. Your chances for a successful interview, however, are much greater if you take this time to carefully prepare for your contact with the child. In most cases, you will only have one chance to create an environment in which a child will talk with you. For the child's sake, you must make the most of this opportunity. Preparation is the key.

❏ Developmental Considerations

Children are not a generic, homogeneous group. They vary in cognitive ability, language, memory, attention spans, social skills, and emotional maturity. Therefore it is essential for the interviewer to understand the different stages of child development and accordingly mold the interview environment, activities, and questioning. Interviewers cannot assume children understand a word, a question, or an experience in the same way.

Preparation is the key.

An interviewer should carefully observe the child during the rapport/play period (this will be discussed in more detail in Chapter 4). It is here that the interviewer can determine the child's maturity and grasp of various concepts such as:

1. Telling time and dates. (Have the child look at a clock and calendar or relate activities to familiar routines such as meals, bedtime, school, TV, or special events such as Christmas or birthdays—terms like *yesterday, tomorrow,* or *here, there,* may confuse young children.)

2. Sense of measurement. (Ask, "How tall are you?" "How much do you weigh?")

3. Numbers. (Ask, "Can you bring me six crayons?" (Do not ask child to count to 20—rote recall does not determine ability to understand numerical concepts.)

4. Causal relationships. (Note statements such as "The picture fell off the wall, and then there was an earthquake" and "The dog barked and the garbageman stopped at our house.")

5. Perspective. (It is difficult for children under 8 years old to see things from another's point of view. "What did Aunt Betty think of your new dress?" may be a difficult question for young children.)

It is from these observations that the interviewer establishes the child's "developmental baseline." This is important for two main reasons:

1. It establishes a reference point for the interviewer. For example, if the child begins to talk baby-talk when asked questions about a particular person or event, it may depict regression and anxiety that are consistent with sexual abuse. Conversely, if the child uses words or phrases that

are more advanced or complex than the developmental baseline, it could indicate outside/adult influence by the offender.

2. It helps the interviewer create a developmentally sensitive interview—gearing the conversation to the child's level of understanding.

Interview questions can be formed to enhance communication in the following ways:

1. Use simple, short sentences.
2. Use one- or two-syllable words.
3. Use terms/words you heard the child use (avoid words like *victim, abuse, juvenile*).
4. Begin with general, open-ended questions ("Tell me what happened") and then get more specific ("You said you were watching TV? What TV show were you watching?").
5. Avoid vague references to time, such as "last month," "yesterday."
6. Avoid double positives: "You liked that horse ride, didn't you?" or "..., isn't that true?"
7. Avoid double negatives: "Didn't you think you were not supposed to tell?"
8. Use names when possible rather than gender pronouns such as *he* or *she.*
9. Watch the child for nonverbal cues indicating confusion. Do not assume the child will say, "I don't understand your question."
10. Be literal and concrete in your word selection (e.g., do not say, "The private parts of the body are what's underneath a swimsuit"—a child may not disclose abuse because he or she did not have a swimsuit on at the time).
11. When using the child's terms, clarify their meaning. Young children use words such as *daddy* to mean all adult men or tall males, just as they say *ball* for any round toy, or *dog* for any furry animal.

The following is a list of some age-appropriate behaviors for children (Levy, Kalinowski, Markovic, Pittman, & Ahart, 1991):

2½ to 3 Years of Age

1. Some ability to comprehend. Can answer yes-no questions.
2. Can recognize some primary colors, but are confused by shades.
3. Can disclose where an incident occurred.

4. Can demonstrate meaning of *behind, over, under, on top of.*
5. Know many of the parts of the body.
6. Difficulty with the complex concepts of truth and lies, although often know consequence if they tell a lie.
7. May not be able to "name" perpetrator, especially if stranger.
8. Time is a difficult concept.
9. Curious about dolls' body parts and openings.
10. Lack of sexual knowledge.
11. Short attention span.
12. Have difficulty with gender pronouns, such as *he* or *she.*

4 to 6 Years of Age

1. More articulate, can tell and demonstrate information.
2. Better at answering questions regarding time.
3. Difficulty in separating multiple abuse incidents.
4. Lots of imitating behaviors.
5. Fearful of threats made by offender.
6. Can be coached by an adult to tell interviewer specific information.
7. Can conceptualize between fantasy and reality.
8. Know gender pronouns.

The important principle to remember with all children is that they need a context for their words—a personal experience to help them understand and construct rules for how the world operates. Children, just like adults, have fantasies and can make up stories. But a trained interviewer, sensitive to child development, can determine if the child's information is in context. Asking age-appropriate questions, listening carefully to what is said, and critically watching what is demonstrated will enhance the interviewer's ability to deal with young children.

4

The Interview: Establishing Rapport

The goal of the interview is to create an opportunity to talk and to gather information with minimal trauma for the child.

When you first meet with a child who may have been sexually abused, it is extremely important that you establish a level of trust and communication. Children who have consistently been manipulated by adults do not readily trust other adults. Before an effective interview can take place, you will need to earn the child's trust and establish the rapport necessary for good communication.

Many factors influence whether you are successful in establishing this rapport: how you introduce yourself, your level of comfort when talking with the child, how you respond to the child's comments, the care with which you ask questions, and the manner in which you respond to the child's emotions and concerns. Described below are some guidelines that will help you establish the necessary trust and communication with a child who is a possible victim of sexual assault.

❑ General Rapport Building

It is important that you first try to relieve any anxiety a child may have about "being in trouble." To do this, begin with a clear message about who you are and why you are there. Be specific and use words the child can understand. For example, start by identifying your professional role and where you work:

- "I'm a police officer and I work for the Springfield Police Department."
- "I'm a child protective services worker and I work for Benson County Children's Services."
- "I'm a lawyer and I work for the District Attorney's Office."

Follow this information with your name, and then elaborate more specifically on what you do in your job.

- "My name is Gretchen Smith. My job is to help children and their families."
- "People call me Detective Jones. Part of my job is to help children who have questions or problems."

Be sure to communicate to the child that he or she is not in trouble. State as carefully as possible that you have come to talk because someone was concerned about him or her. When talking with young children, ask if they know what a police officer or child protective services worker does. Let the child describe this in his or her own words. Then explain that part of your job is talking with children, just as you are doing right now. Help the child to understand that talking with children is something you do all the time: "I talk to lots and lots of children. Last week I even talked to someone else in this same school."

Once you have helped the child understand who you are, try to encourage the child to share something about himself or herself. Ask about personal interests and other subjects the child might feel safe in discussing:

- What grade is the child in?
- Who is the teacher?

- What is the name of a favorite TV show?
- What game or song does the child like best?

When the child shares some information or indicates a preference, show respect and interest. Respond by sharing some of your own preferences or ask the child to tell you more.

During this introductory exchange, your goal is to show the child that you are an adult who can be trusted and who will listen. Try to be patient, and try to answer all the child's questions honestly. Be aware of your physical style and presence. Get down to the eye level of the child, such as sitting or kneeling. Give the child the option to sit in your chair. Being at a 45-degree angle to the child is comfortable for conversation. Sit approximately 24 in. to 36 in. from the child or whatever seems most comfortable. Sitting too close can make a child feel intimidated. Being too far away can be perceived as being unconcerned, distant, or unapproachable. Never conduct an interview from across a desk or table. The child will be watching your body language, as well as the expressions on your face. Likewise, watch the child's body actions (e.g., eye contact, folded arms, crossed legs, tight or slumped shoulders). The child will also be listening to your voice and to the words you choose.

- Do you really know how to talk with children?
- Do you use words that match the child's age and level of under-standing?
- Are you really listening to the child's responses?
- Do you give the child an opportunity to ask questions, or enough time to respond to your questions?
- Can you be trusted?

This rapport-building conversation is very important to the child. It is a time when many decisions will be made about whether you are an adult who cares and listens. Try not to appear hurried or anxious about time. Clear information about who you are, what your job is, and why you are there will help to establish trust. Providing information about yourself and showing a willingness to learn something about the child will help to open lines of communication on a

personal level. Spending too much time discussing general information, however, may cause the child to wonder what the interview is
all about and why you are really there. This may have an unintended
effect of increasing the child's anxiety, especially if it results in a
feeling of being manipulated.

People who interview very young children find it is easiest to
establish rapport and open communication during a "free play" time
period that could take up to 30 minutes. Interviewers can observe the
child and evaluate verbal, emotional, and cognitive ability. You may
want to consider observing the child play or interact with a familiar
person to get a baseline of verbal output. If the child becomes very
quiet or nonverbal with the interviewer but was quite talkative with
the familiar person, more time should be spent on rapport building.
Likewise, it is important not to immediately begin using tools on the
assumption that the child is nonverbal. Rapport building can also be
a natural segue into the main part of the interview.

❏ Helping the Child to Volunteer Information

Interviewing a child who may have been sexually abused requires
a fair degree of patience and considerable tact. Although you may
have very convincing evidence that the child has been sexually
assaulted, you cannot actually discuss the suspected abuse until the
child brings up the subject. Even then, you must avoid asking questions that assume information that the child has not yet shared. If the
interviewer talks to the child without knowing any background
information or the alleged abuse, then the danger of contaminating
the interview by accidentally asking prejudiced questions is minimized. A critical component of the rapport-building stage is that of
helping the child to volunteer information about past sexual abuse.
What you are looking for is some reasonable indication from the child
that there is, in fact, cause to be concerned.

To begin your interview, use transition statements or questions.
Ask the child if he or she knows why you are there. Many children
who have been abused will simply state that you are there to talk

about the abuse and begin by giving you some basic information, such as "You're here to talk about what my brother does to me." Continue the discussion whenever the child gives you an opening. If the child expresses confusion or no opinion, you will need to explore further. Another transition question might be, "Can you tell me what you told your teacher?"

The following sequence of activities is effective in helping children to raise the topic of sexual abuse, thus giving you the opportunity to probe further.

❏ Creating a Favorite/ Least Favorite Things List

Begin by asking the child to verbally list all the people with whom he or she lives, and then clarify the child's relationship with each person (e.g., mother, stepfather, sister, mom's boyfriend, grandfather). Once this list has been created, ask the child to tell you what he or she likes most and least about living with each person.

- "What is your favorite thing about living with your Dad?"
- "What is your least favorite thing about living with your Dad?"

The child may provide an opening to the problem of sexual abuse by suggesting something that is uncomfortable about a particular person. If so, pursue this opening by asking the child to explain or describe this feeling. If you have reason to believe that the offender is someone outside the family, for example, a neighbor, this "Favorite/Least Favorite Things List" should be modified accordingly.

Even if the child does not indicate any major concerns at this point, the information obtained in this activity will be helpful throughout your investigation. Perhaps later, the child will reveal that one of these people has indeed been sexually abusive but may also want to convince you that the person is really okay or loving. The Favorite/ Least Favorite Things List helps you to understand and support the child's positive feelings toward the abuser. The favorite things the child mentions can also be helpful in identifying how the abuser gained and maintained access to the child. Once created, the Favorite/ Least Favorite Things List becomes another piece of background information and may help you to ask appropriate questions at a later time in the interview.

❏ Problem Solving

If the above activity does not elicit any information about sexual abuse, a "problem-solving" format should be tried. Start by reminding the child that your job is to help children and families who have problems. Then ask the child if there is any problem with which he or she could use your help. If nothing is suggested, ask what kinds of problems the child is already good at solving on his or her own. If necessary, offer some examples like

- "What if your shoe comes untied?"
- "What if you fall off your bike and hurt yourself?"
- "How do you cross a busy street safely?"

You can then ask the child to describe problems that are slighty bigger and therefore might need a friend's help or a family's help. (Example: Your dog ran away from home). Finally, ask the child to indicate what problems might need the help of someone from outside the family. (Example: You broke your arm.) It is important to reassure the child that everyone has problems and that everyone occasionally needs help from other people. Reiterate that it is your job to help people with their problems and that you would like to help with any problem the child might have. Then ask again if there is a problem with which you can help. At this point, many children will begin to open up. For example,

Child: Sometimes I have a problem with my Dad.

If so, your next response should be something like:

Interviewer: What about your Dad?

Child: He does things.
Interviewer: What kinds of things?

This may be the opening for which you have been waiting. If the child continues to share his or her concerns, you have now launched into a formal interview. If the child fails to offer more details, you may wish to share with the child some of the information contained in the report or complaint, without revealing who made the report or suggesting any sexual activity. This often prompts a child to elaborate on the shared information, because there is the feeling that you probably already know what is going to be said.

> *It is extremely important to be careful not to lead the child.*

With either of these "problem-solving" prompts, it is extremely important to be careful not to lead the child. This is a danger when suggesting any new information or giving examples from reports. It is generally better to remind the child you were not there and don't know what happened.

❏ Discussion of Privacy

A discussion about privacy is often helpful if a child remains quiet and untalkative. Because this topic can sometimes be construed as directing the interview, you will need to be very careful not to suggest or imply to the child that anything inappropriate or illegal has occurred. *Privacy* can be a big word for many kids and have many different interpretations based upon their home life. Explain that *privacy* means being able to be alone when you want to be. Then ask the child if there are times when he or she likes to have privacy. In which rooms at home can they have privacy? What do they like to do privately? Follow up this discussion with a question about each person living in the child's home. Ask how each person responds to the child's wish for privacy. This frequently opens a door to the discussion of sexual abuse.

❏ Discussion of Safety Rules

If you still have not been able to elicit any information that supports the report of suspected abuse, try asking the child about his or her knowledge of safety rules. Ask what the child has learned about fire safety, bike safety, personal safety, telephone safety, walking to and from school, and so on. Encourage the child to list safety rules for each topic you suggest. It is important not to imply anything inappropriate or to attempt to provide safety instruction. The goal is to create an opportunity for the child to talk. When the topic of personal safety is discussed, information about sexual abuse may be uncovered. Any leads the child gives you, including verbal or physical discomfort with the topic, should be pursued. During this discussion, try to act as if personal safety is equally as important to you as the other forms of safety. Your tone of voice should be comforting yet matter of fact whether you are discussing fire, bike, or personal safety.

The above sequence of activities and topics for discussion will usually help a child to volunteer information about sexual abuse if abuse has occurred. A failure to gather any information that might substantiate the report of sexual abuse may mean that no abuse has occurred. It may also mean, however, that the child is still afraid to talk. If this happens, it is best not to pressure the child further. Experience has shown that when a child is not ready to talk about an abusive incident, a pressured or forced interview may result in information that is later recanted.

Show concern and let the child know you will remain in contact. Clearly explain that you are available to talk if the child has concerns he or she would like to share. If you plan to try an interview again, tell the child you will come back in the near future so that you can talk some more. Identify a support person whom the child should contact if he or she wishes to talk further with you. Be very specific about who this support person is and that this person will call you if contacted. Identify the person clearly, both by name and by relationship to the child—for example, "Your teacher, Mr. Burton, knows how to reach me" or "Grandma Smith has my telephone number and can help you reach me." Often a child will go to this support person not long after your initial interview.

❑ **Important Points to Emphasize**

Throughout the rapport-building phase of the interview, you will want to emphasize several key concepts.

1. It is often helpful if you frequently remind the child of your role. Emphasize and reemphasize that your job is to talk to children in order to help them with their problems.

2. Continually let the child know that you talk to lots of children and that you understand their fears and concerns. Every time you reclarify this information, you are reminding the child that you are an adult with whom children have talked to and trusted with their problems. Try to help the child understand that other children have had the same problems and the same fears. This identification with other children helps the child feel less alone and helps to establish you as someone who can help.

3. Be sure the child understands that whatever is said in the interview, you will share the information only with people who need to know in order to help solve the problem. Never lie to the child about what to expect. Provide enough information for a child so he or she feels like a partner yet not so much that it is cumbersome, frightening, or irrelevant for this point in the investigation. The assurance of confidentiality and the discussion of the limits of this confidentiality are crucial to establishing rapport with children.

❑ **Responding to the
Child's Emotions and Questions**

When a child you are interviewing discloses sexual abuse, he or she will often only offer a small portion of the information in order to see how you respond. This effort at disclosure may trigger an emotional response from the child. Some children cry, some fidget or become hyperactive. Some get angry. Some may try to "escape" by changing the topic or saying they need to go to the bathroom. They may withdraw, become aggressive, or use avoidance or distracting tactics. The most appropriate reaction for you is to acknowledge what you are seeing. This may be the most critical point in the interview as the child decides whether to risk continuing to talk about the abuse or remain silent. If you are able to respond genuinely to the child's fears and concerns, the child may decide you are a person who can be trusted. If you do not show concern, and appear interested only in "getting the facts," you will not be someone with whom the child chooses to share confidences.

Tell the child what you are observing. For example, you might say, "It looks like you are upset. What are you feeling?" If the child answers, "scared" or "afraid," ask, "What are you afraid of?" or "What do you think is the worst thing that could happen?" As the child states reasons why he or she should not talk with you, address each reason separately. Ask the child who said such things would happen. Then reiterate that other children have had the same fears. Although you cannot guarantee everything will be "all right," help the child understand that not all of the "worst" things will happen either. Also, consider the possibility that nothing sexual happened and that the child's discomfort reflects the inability to say that he or she has been misunderstood or is just uncomfortable with the topic.

Many difficult issues tend to surface at this point: the feeling of being responsible for the abuse, the shame of participating, the betrayal of the mother's trust. It is most appropriate to handle these issues in therapy. However, you may wish to help the child understand that what happened was not his or her fault. If the child cries, acknowledge that sometimes it is hard to share this kind of information and that it is all right to cry. Reassure the child that you will help try to solve any problems he or she may have.

If the child asks questions, be honest. For example, a question about whether the offender will get in trouble should not be answered with "We only want to help." Tell the child honestly that you do not make those decisions—it will be left to the judge or court to decide what happens to the offender. If the child is concerned about being placed in a foster home, explain that this is a possibility but that you must know what happened in order to determine what is necessary. Talk about the need for all children to feel safe and comfortable, and then explain that your goal is to help bring about this feeling. If the child asks what will happen next, explain the next step in the process but avoid describing everything that will happen over the next several months.

When you sense that the child is calming down or that the critical questions in the child's mind have been answered, try to bring the interview back on topic. One way to do this is to introduce some of the interview tools you brought, such as paper and crayons. If the child has mentioned where the sexual abuse occurred, try to get the child to draw a simple picture or diagram of the location. If no location has been named, ask the child to draw his or her house. To help children understand that you want a floor plan of their house, request that they "draw a picture of your house as if you were above it, looking down." Another way to get this concept across is to suggest an imaginary helicopter ride during which you "hover" over the top of the child's house and look down inside. Although the drawing you get may not be to scale, this method will usually work, even with young children. The child's picture will help you to understand the basic layout of the house and the location of doors and other outside entrances. Ask the child to explain the drawing when it is completed, pointing out the front door, back door, walkways, and so on.

Following the guidelines in this chapter will help you develop the skills and sensitivity necessary to establish rapport with the children you are asked to interview. If you begin an interview with the methods suggested, chances are much greater that you will conduct a successful interview. Try to keep in mind the little things that may make a child feel safe and comfortable. Get down physically to the child's level and work hard at projecting a relaxed but concerned manner. Be patient and show that you are willing to listen to anything the child wishes to share. Answer the child's questions carefully and honestly, while also supporting the right for the child to be emotional about what has happened. Always try to offer clarification, assistance, and sensitive support.

5

The Interview:
Establishing Incident Details

Once the child has given you an indication that sexual abuse has occurred, you have formally entered the interviewing stage. That is, your goal now becomes one of gathering detailed information about the abuse and about the conditions under which it happened. Even though you are no longer primarily interested in establishing rapport, keep in mind that you will be more successful in obtaining information if you are able to maintain an environment in which the child feels comfortable.

Interviewing tools, such as anatomical dolls, puppets, or drawings, may or may not be needed in gathering information from the child. If not, the interviewer should move from rapport building to asking questions and gathering information surrounding the alleged abusive incident. The same general guidelines, such as not asking leading or suggestive questions, should be followed. If anatomical dolls are needed, the steps outlined here should be helpful as to when and how the dolls should be used.

❏ Introducing the Anatomical Dolls

The anatomical dolls are designed to be used when a child demonstrates some difficulty or embarrassment in describing the sexual
abuse that has occurred. They may be appropriate whenever there is
a language barrier, such as with mentally retarded or non-English-
speaking adults and children. However, not all children or alleged
victims will need the aid of the dolls. For instance, some boys do not
like to use dolls. Do not insist upon their usage if it is unnecessary.
When introducing the anatomical dolls to a child, explain that you
brought some dolls that help you when talking with children. Do not
refer to the dolls as your "special friends," because that is a lure or
term often used by offenders. Communicate that the dolls are yours
but that the child may hold and touch them while you are together.
Stating clearly that they are your dolls will help the child understand
that they are not being offered as a bribe, that you will take them with
you when you leave, and that you are not a scary adult because you
have dolls.

Generally, the anatomical dolls are not used during rapport building. To avoid the risk of contaminating or biasing the interview, or
the appearance thereof, it may be best to wait until the child has
indicated that sexual abuse has occurred before offering the dolls as
an aid to explaining the sexual details of what has happened. One of
the reasons for this is that use of anatomical dolls during interviews
has been challenged in several court systems. It has been argued that
the dolls are suggestive of sexual activity because of their sexual body
parts, thus leading to behaviors that arouse suspicion of sexual abuse
when none may have occurred. Although most professionals in the
field refute this argument, it is best to act cautiously (which may
include introducing the dolls clothed). Remember, offer the dolls
only after a child you are interviewing has provided an indication of
sexual abuse and has exhibited some difficulty in communicating
what occurred.

Before removing the anatomical dolls from their carrying sack, or
from a nearby chair or shelf, explain to the child that the dolls are
different from other dolls. Indicate that they have body parts, including sexual parts, just like real people. You may choose to introduce

the dolls either with or without clothing, although most interviewers prefer to introduce the dolls clothed. When the dolls are presented without clothing, the sexual body parts are immediately visible. A few children may exhibit some surprise or embarrassment, but this usually passes. In some circumstances, you may have reason to believe that clothes, or perhaps their removal, are important details in the alleged incident. If so, have clothing available or present the dolls dressed. Allow the child to dress or undress the dolls and show you what happened.

❑ Body Parts Inventory

Let the child get the dolls and explore them. Many children will stick their fingers in the various holes, pull on the penis, or try to see if the penis fits into the vagina, anus, or mouth. This may be normal exploratory behavior, and is not to be considered evidence of sexual abuse *in and of itself*. Listen carefully, however, to what the child says while exploring the dolls. Many children will say nothing. Others may begin to share details about previous sexual activity. Be aware that it may be necessary to differentiate between abusive touching and basic hygiene touching. Likewise, it may become evident that the child has been exposed to pornography. Although what children do with the dolls may not be significant by itself, what they say might be. For example, in one case a 5-year-old girl who was playing with the penis of the adult male doll said, "Glue comes out the end of his thing. I don't like it. It's sticky on my tummy," and "It smells like fish." This information, based upon sensory experience of touch and smell, is not likely to be known from watching pornography or regular hygiene practices.

Remember, the interviewer's job is to listen, not teach.

When you feel the child has had adequate time to look at and explore each of the dolls, have the child pick one out to talk about. It does not matter which doll you start with, for you will eventually talk about them all. Ask the child if the doll has a name. Then ask the child names for parts of the body by pointing to the doll and saying, "What do you call this?" or "What is the name of that part?" Begin with parts of the body that are not considered sexual (e.g., arm or leg) and then alternate back and forth between naming sexual and nonsexual parts. Always repeat what the child says and use the names provided by the child in subsequent conversation. Do not correct the child and do not volunteer different names for the body parts. When a child offers a slang term such as *pussy* or *cock,* ask the child in a nonjudgmental tone where that name was learned or who suggested that name for the body part. Take care not to sound as if the term used is "dirty" or incorrect. When you have completed naming the body parts on one doll, pick up another doll, repeating the same process until all body parts have been discussed. Remember, the interviewer's job is to listen, not teach.

Some interviewers may feel more comfortable doing the body parts inventory with drawings. This can be useful if the child writes the names for the body parts on the paper. It assists the interviewer in remembering the child's terms and may be good documentation for court.

To establish a child's ability to discriminate between the dolls, hold up two dolls of the same sex, such as a female adult and child. Ask the child if there are any differences between the two. Most children will comment on the difference in size, saying one is taller. Others may point out differences in eye or hair color. If you continue to ask the same question, a child may eventually show you that one doll has pubic hair, developed breasts, or large genitals and the other doesn't. Follow this observation with a question as to what this means. Most children, even quite young children, will be able to tell you that the doll with the pubic hair is "older." Although this information is not particularly critical, it can be very helpful in demonstrating the child's ability to distinguish detail. You will have greater confidence in the child's subsequent descriptions, and the information may help to enhance the child's competency as a witness if this case goes to court.

Some interviewers do not ask very young children which doll is a male and which is a female. Although most children are clear about their own sexual identity at a very young age, they do not always see dolls as having a specific sex. Some children think dressing a doll in a dress makes the doll a girl and boy's clothes make a doll male. An incorrect answer to your question could consequently be used in court to make the child appear incompetent as a witness. Therefore it may be better not to ask the question.

❑ Using the Dolls to Gather Information

Once you have learned the terms used by the child for various parts of the body, you are ready to move into the information-gathering phase. If the child is unable to simply "tell" you what happened, you may now want to use the dolls to obtain specific details. Remind the child of the information given prior to introducing the dolls and then indicate you would like the child to show you what happened using the dolls. Ask the child to pick a doll to represent himself or herself. Do not use the word *pretend* or say, "Let's play like this is you." You want this to be a factual reenactment, not a make-believe game.

By this time, the child may have given you the name of the abuser. Ask the child more open-ended questions. If there is reluctance to talk or the child is vague or unclear, ask the child to pick a doll to "represent" or "be" the person named as the abuser. "Pick a doll to be Uncle John." As discussed earlier, it is important to be sure the child understands representational play. Do not be concerned if the child initially picks a doll of the wrong sex. Frequently the child will recognize the mistake when trying to demonstrate what happened and will change dolls. If not, you might gently ask if the doll has the right body parts to show what happened, but do not suggest that the child exchange dolls. Keep in mind that it is what the child says with the dolls that is most important. If the child is nonverbal, watch facial expressions and body language as the child demonstrates with the dolls. Once these selections have been made, ask the child if the other dolls are needed or if they should be put away in their carrying sack or set aside.

Again ask the child to show you what happened. It may be important to re-dress the dolls before the demonstration begins. The interviewer cannot assume there was nudity of the child or abuser. The child may choose to have one or more of the dolls sitting on his or her lap, or the child may choose to carry the dolls around the room. Regardless of the method used, it is important to remember that demonstrating something with the dolls is not enough. Specifically ask the child to explain, in words, what is being demonstrated. For example, a child may place the hand of the male doll against the vaginal area of a female doll. Ask the child to tell you what is happening. Give the child the option to whisper it to you if he or she would feel more comfortable. However, be sure to repeat out loud what the child told you. If the child is silent or appears embarrassed, ask a question using the words the child gave you earlier when doing the body parts inventory. For example, you might ask, "Are you putting the hand against the (pussy)?" Additionally, a child may feel more comfortable talking about the dolls in third person. For instance, Susie may say the girl doll is "Susie." If this is the case, every so often clarify with the child whom the doll represents.

Sometimes your willingness to verbalize what is being demonstrated will help the child to open up and start talking again.

If possible, it is best to start talking about the child's first sexual incident with the alleged offender and move to the present chronologically. This progression usually helps the child by allowing the discussion to focus on more distant (and often less scary) incidents first, then building to closer, more recent experiences. Ask the child about the first time something happened with the named offender. Let the child know you want to understand everything that has happened and that other children you have talked to found it easier to start with details of the first time.

Your ability to keep the interview moving (and therefore gather the necessary information) will often depend upon how well you ask follow-up questions. Avoid asking questions that appear to assume the child has finished telling you about an incident. For example, asking, "Is that all that happened?" may indicate you do not expect more to have occurred. Some children will be hesitant to volunteer more information if they feel you have heard enough. Try to ask questions that lead to additional information or to a description of the next incident. After a child has used the dolls to demonstrate and describe a specific experience, ask open-ended, follow-up questions: "What happened next?" Once again, avoid questions that require a "yes" or "no" response. Also, limit your follow-up questions. Too many questions can make the child feel pressured and consequently misinterpret that the interviewer "wants me to tell her/him more."

Very young children may feel the need to hide or not look at you during the interview. Some may do this by turning their back from you or by going behind a piece of furniture. Let the child do this. If you cannot see the dolls, the child will need to describe what is being done with them. As you continue to listen and support the child, he or she will eventually be able to talk with you more directly. If this does not happen, allow the child to remain where he or she is. Gently encourage the child to let you see the dolls while explaining and demonstrating.

As the child describes a particular incident, ask for peripheral information that could be used to help establish the time of the abuse and to establish the child's credibility. Prompt the child to remember details surrounding the time and place for each incident by asking questions such as

- "Where did you live when this happened?" (If the child does not know or remember an address, ask follow-up questions such as "Was it an apartment or a house?" and "What color was it?")
- "What school did you attend?" "Who was your teacher?"
- "What grade were you in?"
- "Who did you live with?" "Was there anyone visiting during this time period?"
- "Do you remember anything special that happened about this time?" "Was it close to any holiday?"

In most cases of sexual abuse, there is an element of secrecy established between the abuser and the victim. This secrecy is one way the abuser retains his or her access to the child. Identifying an element of secrecy in the relationship and uncovering details concerning how this secrecy was maintained can be helpful when trying to validate the child's account in court. To determine how secrecy about the abuse was established and maintained, ask the child what other people said about the abuse—for example, "What did your stepmom think about this?" The child will often respond by indicating that it was a "secret" or that he or she was "told not to tell." Some good follow-up questions at this point are "Who told you not to tell?"

and "What did he (or she) say would happen if you told?" After the element of secrecy has been established, it is important to assure the child that telling was the right thing to do. Communicate that you are glad the child told you and that it is not fair for an adult to ask a child to keep a secret about touching.

Use the dolls throughout the interview as necessary to clarify what the child is trying to explain. But remember, the dolls do not "do" the interview for you. The dolls are merely an aid to understanding what the child is trying to communicate. When you request peripheral information about incidents described, such as dates and locations, the child will frequently continue to do things with the dolls. As you see this happening, ask the child to explain what is happening. Allowing the child to explore the dolls freely, without questions being asked, may also provide useful information. It is not uncommon for this more unstructured exploration to lead to information about additional incidents, or additional abusers. Continue to observe carefully and ask questions as needed to clarify what the child is demonstrating. Victims of sexual abuse may also show some anger or hostility toward one or more of the dolls. It is important to allow the child to express these feelings. Acknowledge to the child that it is okay to feel angry, frustrated, or confused and that other children in the same situation have felt the same way.

How you react to what the child says and does during the interview is extremely important. In general, it is best to underreact whenever possible. A simple "Uh-huh" and a nod are generally effective. Be supportive of the child talking, not necessarily what was or was not said. For instance, "You're doing a good job, Becky. Let's keep talking and working hard." If you suspect the child is lying—for instance, if he or she is overly protective of a person, if the story changes, or if details parallel a TV program—do not be accusatory.

It is best to underreact whenever possible.

Instead, prompt the child to repeat what he or she just said. For example, you might say in a kind, nonjudgmental voice: "Could you tell me about that again? But this time, only tell me the part that really happened, okay?"

Remember, many abuse cases, especially those involving ritualistic abuse, have bizarre circumstances.

Figure 5.1. Avoid Leading Questions During the Interview

Do not show support for the child with hugs, pats on the head, or any similar touching. This could give a confusing, mixed message to the child and appear manipulative to a judge or jury. If a child cries or becomes emotionally upset, ask him or her if there is something you can do or if the child wants a hug. Give the decision and the sense of control about touching to the child.

❏ Avoiding Leading Questions

Always avoid the use of leading and suggestive questions. Leading questions are those that direct the child's response by providing information not yet stated or by including the answer within the question itself. If you ask leading questions during the interview, the information provided by the child cannot be trusted and the whole interview may be suspect. This could ultimately result in the case being dismissed from court. Some examples of leading questions are "Don't you have a problem with your dad?" "Doesn't he touch you down there?" or "Your grandma is worried because your mom's boyfriend tickles your bottom." Each of these questions suggests that something specific has happened to the child or that the child has a problem with a specific person. Questions that elicit a yes or no answer or that provide the child with a limited choice are almost always leading questions: "Did your dad say that?" "Was it red or white?" "Did it feel soft or hard?"

It is difficult to avoid asking leading questions, and in some situations they may be unavoidable. However, leading questions are always subject to be challenged in a legal setting. Try practicing a nonleading interview with a coworker. Select a case on which you are currently working or one you were just assigned. Set up a role-playing situation and practice asking relevant questions. Phrase your questions so that they ask for further information without directing the content of that information. In general, questions that begin with "what," "when," "how," and "who" are good questions to ask. For example, the following are not leading questions:

- "What happened next?"
- "How do you know that is making babies?"
- "Who told you that was called a dick?"
- "What did it look like?"
- "How did it feel?"
- "When did that happen?"
- "Where did that happen?"

As you practice you will learn to rephrase questions before you say them and to monitor yourself throughout the interview.

Another way to avoid asking leading questions is to paraphrase what the child has said and then ask a very general follow-up question. For example, if the child puts the adult male doll's mouth touching the female child doll's vaginal area and says, "He is licking her bottom," you might respond with "It looks like the man is licking the girl's bottom [use child's word here]. Is that what you are showing and explaining to me?" The following is another example of an interchange where the interviewer uses paraphrasing of the child's statements and actions.

The child shows the adult male doll on top of the child doll.

Interviewer: What is happening?
Child: They are sleeping.
Interviewer: Is anything else happening?
Child: He is humping her.
Interviewer: It is hard for me to see this. Can you show me what humping means?

Child demonstrates with the dolls and says, "This thing goes in that thing."

Interviewer: It looks like you are putting the man's thing in the girl's thing. Is that correct?
Child: Yes.
Interviewer: Remind me what you call these parts. A man's thing is . . . .
Child: Penis.
Interviewer: Okay, and a girl's thing is . . . . ?
Child: Private.
Interviewer: Okay, so the man's penis went in the girl's private?
Child: Yes.
Interviewer: How do you know this happened?
Child: Because that is what he did to me.
Interviewer: The man's penis went into your private?
Child: Yes.
Interviewer: How do you know his penis went into your private?
Child: I could feel it and it hurt!
Interviewer: Who was the man?
Child: My dad.

Avoid using multiple-choice questions. This can limit a child's verbal responses, perhaps incorrectly, by restricting options and information. Additionally, an interviewer should not demand that the child tell the truth or threaten or coerce the child with the interviewer's authority or promise, in exchange for the "truth" from the child, that the offender will never do this (awful) thing again. The interviewer is the neutral fact gatherer, not the judge and jury.

Sometimes a child may have difficulty in talking to you in a conversational style. In some cases, the child may ask you to reword your questions so that only a "yes" or "no" answer is required. Tell the child that you cannot do this but that you will try to reword the questions so they are simpler to understand. The child may be too embarrassed with both the questions and the answers. Present an alternative to the child to write down the questions or answers and give them to you. You can then read them out loud and have the child react or respond.

Be cautious if a child seems to answer questions or make statements in a rote fashion. It may mean the child has been coached. Also, a child's negative reactions to your questions may not mean he or she was abused. It could be based on the child's fear, confusion over the question, or anxiety over some extenuating circumstance.

❏ Closing the Interview

When you feel you have gathered as much information as possible from the child and have explored the possibility of other perpetrators, it is time to close the interview. It is important that you do this in a manner that helps the child feel comfortable about having talked with you. This may influence the child's willingness to talk with you in the future and cooperate if the case goes to court. You want to avoid giving the impression that you are only interested in the child as a piece of evidence. Praise the child for helping you and for being able to talk about something that is very personal and hard to discuss. Emphasize to the child that he or she is not to blame for what has happened, and that the blame rests with the abuser.

Review your notes with the child. This will help to ensure that you have documented the narration correctly and reinforce to the child that you value what has been said. Watch the child's physical reaction/body language as you go over the notes. Be open to the notion there may be more than one offender. Explain the next step in the investigative process, but avoid going into detail about what might take place over the next several months. Remember not to make any promises ("This will never happen again") or offer false hope. Be supportive but realistic. Tell the child when you expect to see him or her again. Explain that you will write a report so you can remember what you discussed. In case you forgot anything, you may need to talk to the child again. Likewise, if the child thinks of something he or she wishes to tell you, give the child your phone number as well as identify a "safe" person to contact if there are questions or problems. Whenever possible and if appropriate, try to end the interview with some activity that is pleasant for the child, like discussing a personal interest or hobby.

If the child asks to keep one of the anatomical dolls, remind him or her that the dolls belong to you. Explain that you use the dolls frequently when talking with boys and girls who have problems or need to tell you something. Try to help the child understand that because the dolls assist children in explaining what has happened, you will need the dolls to help other children explain what has happened to them.

❏ **Follow-Up Interviews**

It will probably be necessary to conduct multiple interviews with every child suspected of being a victim of sexual abuse. Multiple interviews, generally a few days apart, are necessary because children are often unable to tell you everything or make a disclosure the first time you meet. These interviews should always be conducted or observed by one of the same people who talked with the child in the initial interview. Two interviews should be the minimum number before writing a report and are often all that is necessary.

At the beginning of a second interview, let the child know why you are meeting again. It may be that you need to confirm information the child shared with you last time or that you need to ask some questions about the child's story. Also there may be another person who needs to hear the information given by the child, such as a prosecutor, a therapist, or an additional investigator. This person may be in the room, observing by a one-way mirror, or may view the videotape at a later point. A second interview allows the interviewer to assess consistency over time in the child's report. This consistency can help strengthen a case and help show that the child will be a credible witness in court.

Follow-up interviews are conducted in a manner similar to initial interviews. Rapport building is usually easier because you are a known person. Whether you use the anatomical dolls during a follow-up interview is determined by the child, so the dolls should be available. Again, if it appears that the child is having difficulty answering your questions, let the child use the dolls to demonstrate and explain. You will often gather more detailed information during the second interview, primarily because the child is more likely to trust you and therefore reveal more intimate details. Follow-up interviews should be closed in a manner similar to the initial interview. Explain to the child the next step in the investigation process and indicate when you expect to see the child again. Cases will need to be referred for more extensive evaluations when the child has not disclosed abuse but there continue to be concerns or "red flag" behaviors or indicators.

❑ **Taking Good Notes**

In order to document the information a child reveals in an interview, you will need to take careful notes. At the beginning of your contact with a child, let him or her know that you will be taking notes throughout the interview. Emphasize that the notes are needed because the information is very important and you need to remember it correctly. Indicate that one of the rules of your job is that you have to write a report. Because you want this report to be accurate, you will need to keep notes. It is also helpful if you remind the child that you talk to lots of children and that taking notes will prevent you from confusing his or her information with that of the other children. Tell the child that you will review your notes with him or her at the end of the interview. Not only will this give you an opportunity to ensure that your notes are correct, it will also help the child to feel some control over the interview and over the content of your notes.

What should be included in your notes? It is best if your notes focus on general trends in the child's story rather than on specific details of the sexual activity. A child's recollection of the details may change over time, and therefore each telling of an incident may bring forth slightly different information. If there is a trial many months after the initial interview and the child's memory of the events is different or faded, a listing of previously recorded details may ultimately be used to discredit the child's testimony.

It is normal for these changes in our memory to occur over time. If you wish to demonstrate this to yourself, try to remember what you had for dinner last night. Now try to remember what you had exactly 1 week ago, then 2 weeks ago. What differences do you notice in the details remembered about each meal? Or ask yourself:

- Were you ever in an accident?
- Have you ever received a serious injury?
- How many times did you have to tell your version of the story?
- Was your story exactly the same each time you told it?
- Did the details change each time you told it?
- Did you find yourself focusing on the details your listener was interested in and glossing over others?

Now try to remember the last time you had consenting, pleasurable sexual relations with someone. Can you recall in detail what happened first, second, third, and so on?

Now try remembering the second-to-last time you had sexual relations with someone.

- How do the details of this experience differ?
- Was it different or the same?

Now try remembering the third-to-last time you had sexual relations.

- Do you remember exactly what happened?
- Is it difficult to keep each of these experiences separate?

It is generally difficult for adults to remember such detail, even when their experiences were enjoyable and one would think they would want to remember details. Conversely, a victim of a nonconsensual sexual experience wants to forget the fear and confusion and pain. Therefore the child often does forget or repress such detail. It is difficult for children—especially when the experiences are ones that they would rather not remember.

Children generally recall less information than adults, but what they do remember is quite accurate. Additionally, children's memory errors tend to be those of omission of information rather than commission of errors. Therefore open-ended questions such as "What happened next?" or "Tell me what happened" should provide an opportunity for accurate reporting of details. Because the information may still be incomplete, prompts by the interviewer, using words the child has already used, should assist in getting at those omitted details.

Record information that establishes a pattern of abuse such as the progression of sexual activity over time (because many offenders "groom" their victims, starting with simple touching and escalating to more intimate sexual behaviors), age of the child when abuse situations occurred, and a general time frame for the incidents. Document whom the child identified as an offender and record information that may be corroborated by other people, such as locations where the abuse took place, references to special events that occurred at the time of the incidents, and recurring habits of the offender.

Some details should be recorded, such as statements the child remembers having been made by the offender. For example, the child might indicate,"He said that getting undressed was our secret" or "He said people would think I was a bad kid." Other direct quotes that should be recorded are those that help document a child's attempts to tell someone about the abuse. For example, a child might say, "I always told Mom and Dad I didn't want Jimmy to babysit at night," or "I told my sister to stay away from Uncle Syd—especially if he was drinking." Direct quotes such as these are helpful when you talk with others who may corroborate the child's story.

When the child is demonstrating something with the anatomical dolls, take care to write down both the child's physical actions and the verbal explanations. For example, you might record: "Child laid adult male on top of female child—stomach to stomach—put penis into vagina and moved male doll up and down. Child said, 'They're humping.' I asked, 'How do you know that is called humping?' Child said, 'Dad said, that's how.' 'When did he say that?' 'When he humped me!' " Again, be careful not to include too much extraneous detail in your notes, just enough to document the child's actions and explanations. Additionally, do not hinder the momentum of the child's disclosure by your note taking. Always be aware of the fact that writing can be distracting and that the child may think you are not listening. Always be willing to stop your note taking at any time.

If a child objects strongly to your taking notes, try to make an arrangement that is acceptable. If you are working in a team, have one team member talk to the child and the other take notes. This is generally much less disruptive. If an acceptable arrangement cannot be agreed upon, respect the child's wishes about note taking. Be sure, however, that right after the interview you write down the information obtained.

Notes are a valuable resource to you as the investigation proceeds. Use your notes to help you recall an initial interview with a child prior to a follow-up interview or an appearance in court. Notes from interviews will be used as the basis for any report you are required to write. Take care to document your interviews carefully, but avoid binding the child to only one way of describing the sexual contact that occurred. Being open, neutral, and objective throughout the investigation is essential, even after the initial interview. Failure to observe this caution may result in your being the best witness for the defense!

❏ Videotaping

An increasing number of agencies are videotaping interviews with child sexual abuse victims. Because this is a controversial practice, agencies should carefully weigh the advantages and disadvantages of videotaping before implementing this procedure.

If videotaping interviews is to be incorporated as a regular investigative practice, guidelines should be written and agreed upon by the local law enforcement agencies, child protective services, and the district attorney/prosecutor's office. In order to avoid unnecessary legal battles, you may want the local public defender or a defense bar representative to review the policy.

The advantages of videotaping include:

1. Reducing the need for multiple interviews with the child and thus reducing trauma
2. Being able to review the tape with a multidisciplinary team or with other professionals who might observe things differently than the interviewer
3. Providing concrete, visual evidence of what the child said and did (e.g., demonstrated with the dolls, turned red, got embarrassed, fidgeted)
4. Establishing a record that indicates you were careful not to lead the child when asking questions
5. Creating a persuasive tool to show the alleged offender—many a confession or plea has occurred after the offender has watched an interview tape—thus avoiding the stress on the child and the expense of the case going to trial
6. Making a permanent record on videotape that might eventually be accepted in place of courtroom testimony, sparing the child a court-room confrontation with the abuser (this may require legislation to be enacted)

There are several disadvantages to videotaping interviews. They include:

1. Many jurisdictions cannot afford, or do not have the space to set up, a comfortable interview room for children that is conducive for filming (camera angle, flexibility, sound, lighting). Because video equipment is becoming more sophisticated, easier to operate, and less expensive, this may not be as much of an issue as it once was.
2. There are limitations on your choice of a location for an initial interview because equipment may be in only one location.
3. The details recorded on tape and the details shared in court may differ. The defense attorney may claim that prior inconsistent statements were made. They may be used to call into question the child's credibility.
4. The microphone, tape recorder, camera, or other equipment may make the child and interviewer uncomfortable.
5. The recording may be inaudible or may malfunction in some way, thus losing valuable information.

As in a nontaped interview, the adult interviewer should always repeat aloud exactly what the child says. Because children's voices are often soft and high-pitched, the audio portion of the videotape may not be able to pick up all of what the child is saying.

❏ Interviewing the Very Young Child

Gathering information from a child between the ages of 2 and 4 can be very difficult. Some children in this age range can verbally communicate very well; others are still speaking only in one- or two-word utterances. If you have information that would suggest a child in this age group has been sexually abused, there are some differences in the basic interviewing procedure that should be observed. The primary difference occurs when you interview other people who know the child or might be able to provide you with information concerning the abuse. You should always try to talk to the person who reported the suspected abuse, regardless of the child's age. But if the child is very young, it is best to talk to additional acquaintances of the child before the interview. With older children, this is usually done after the interview as a means of validating the child's information (see Chapter 5).

The purpose of gathering this additional information on young children is to assist you in preparing for the interview and in establishing a comfortable environment for the child. When selecting people to talk to, take care not to alert anyone who might try to hide the child from you or describe you as someone to be feared. In general, it is best to try to interview all the people close to the child (e.g., relatives, neighbors, day care providers), with the exception of anyone suspected of being the offender.

The second major difference in interviewing procedures for young children is the location of the interview. Once you have gathered all the information possible, ask a person with whom the child is comfortable to bring the child to your office. Prepare a room in which you can spend some time with the child. In addition to the usual interviewing tools, you will want to have some toys and games that are at the appropriate developmental level for the child. Have the toys, your interviewing tools, and the anatomical dolls placed about the room when the child arrives. The dolls do not need to be in a prominent spot, but should be readily available and visible to the child.

When you interview a young child, you may choose to have a trusted adult come into the room. For extremely young children, this may ease their anxiety over being in a new place talking to a strange person. This trusted adult should understand, however, that he or she is not to participate in the interview. This includes making verbal comments or nonverbal reactions such as rolling his or her eyes or other judgmental facial reactions. If the child appears willing to go with you and be interviewed alone, then try this first. Young children may appear nervous for a few minutes, but often relax when they see an inviting room and new toys with which to play. In general, the decision about whether to include the trusted adult will depend, in large part, on the relationship of this adult to the child and the child's apparent comfort in new places.

Using the information you have gathered as a foundation for the case, try to engage the child in talking about activities that are peripheral to the suspected abuse. Because of the child's age, your questions may need to focus on a particular person or activity. Be careful, however, not to suggest anything sexual. Depending on the information gathered, you might want to begin your interview with questions such as:

- "What did you do when Uncle Bob visited?"
- "What did you do at Mommy's house?"
- "What did you do at Daddy's house?"
- "What did you do when your babysitter was over?"
- "What kind of games did you play?"

The questions are more focused than with older children; however, they still must not be suggestive or leading. If the child alludes to any form of sexual activity, ask him or her to show you with the anatomical dolls. Remember to continually establish through questions that the child understands representational play.

At the beginning of your interaction, it is likely that the child will discover the dolls and explore them. If the child does overtly sexual things with the dolls, such as sexual intercourse or oral sodomy, this activity may serve as an opening for asking appropriate, nonleading questions. Keep in mind, though, that what the child does with the dolls is not an automatic indication of sexual abuse and should be accompanied by some verbal explanation, however minimal. If the child does something such as putting the penis into the vagina and moving the dolls up and down, ask questions like:

> *What the child does with the dolls is not an automatic indication of sexual abuse.*

- "What is happening?"
- "Where have you seen this?"
- "Who told you this was 'making babies'?"

The information you get from the child may be sparse, but probably relevant and to the point. An example of this was a case involving a 2-year-old girl who was suspected of being sexually abused by her father on a weekend visit. The suspicion arose when, upon her return from a visit, she became very interested in her brother's penis. She pulled his pants down and attempted to put her mouth on his penis.

She was brought to the Child Protective Services Division office and was interviewed. When asked if she had visited her Daddy, she responded with an affirmative nod. A follow-up question concerning what she did when visiting Daddy brought no response. When asked to draw a picture of visiting Daddy, she scribbled all over a piece of paper. When asked if she had played games with Daddy, she again nodded her head and said, "Uh-huh." The little girl then wandered around the room and looked over the toys, games, and stuffed animals. When she encountered the anatomical dolls, she picked up the adult male doll and brought it to the interviewer. Pointing to the penis she said, "Me bite," and then bit the penis of the doll. When the interviewer asked who the doll was, she said, "Daddy." The interviewer asked, "Who do you bite?" and she responded, "Daddy." If the interviewer had asked the question, "You bite Daddy?" he or she should also have asked an equal "check" question such as "You bite Mommy?"

Gathering information from a child in this age group is more difficult than gathering information from older children. Furthermore, you will have greater difficulty qualifying a very young child as a competent witness. The information you gather, however, can be critical in any attempt to protect the child from future abuse. In addition, what you learn from the child may be supported by medical evidence and witnesses. As with all interviews, considerable caution must be exercised to avoid leading questions or to suggest, in any way, that something sexual has happened.

6

Going to Trial

❑ Preparing the Child for the Courtroom

Preparing the child for courtroom testimony begins with the initial interview. If the child feels, from the very first interview, that he or she can talk openly and be believed, then you have laid the groundwork for effective courtroom testimony. If not, the child may become a reluctant witness.

❑ Explaining the Legal Process

Always keep the child advised of what the next step will be in the legal process. Unexpected appointments may undermine the child's confidence in you and the legal system. The child may begin to question his or her ability to survive in this strange, new environment. Use language the child can understand when explaining the

legal procedures. For instance, some young children might understand better if you talk about "rules" instead of "laws." Children
recognize that they must follow
rules at home or school, whether
they like them or not. Explain that
grown-ups have rules to follow too.

*Use language the child
can understand.*

Be sure that each child has an adult
with him or her throughout the court process. Ideally, this adult
should be a person known to the child from the beginning of the case,
such as a caseworker or court-appointed advocate. This provides
security as well as continuity for the child during a new and poten-
tially stressful experience.

There are a few books written for children, such as *My Day at the
Courthouse* (Dooley, 1985), that help explain the legal process and
what to expect. The use of picture illustrations and a story makes
children much less fearful. The unknown becomes known, unfamiliar terms become defined, and children can visualize what to expect.

❏ Familiarity and Protocol

Visiting the courtroom and meeting with the prosecutor ahead of
time are essential. First, visit the room where the child will be testifying
(e.g., the juvenile courtroom, the criminal courtroom, the grand jury
room). Next, let the child walk around the room, sit anywhere, and
practice talking both with and without the microphone. Explain the
role of each person who will be in the courtroom (e.g., court reporter,
defense attorney, bailiff, judge, prosecutor, jury). Let the child know
where each person will sit and who will be asking questions. Make
sure the child goes through an interview with the prosecutor in the
courtroom at least once. With the prosecutor or yourself, walk through
the procedures of a competency hearing, a sample direct examination, and a sample cross-examination. As you go through this practice session, be sure to use any tools you will be using the day the
child is in court (e.g., dolls, maps, photos).

Let the child know the basic rules of the courtroom. These rules
include always answering honestly, never guessing at an answer, and

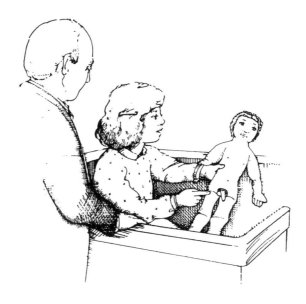

Figure 6.1. The Dolls Can Be a Useful Demonstration Aid in Court

always letting the attorneys and judge know if a question is confusing or cannot be heard. Role play such a situation so the child can feel comfortable about saying, "I don't understand your question. I'm confused."

Give the child a sense of control in each stage of the legal process by offering choices. For instance, let the child pick what he or she wears to court. Help the child to understand what would be appropriate to wear and then let the child decide. Let the child choose whom he or she wants to have in the courtroom during the child's testimony. Having a selected support person often reassures the child by giving him or her someone "safe" to look at.

❏ **Competency Hearings**

In most states, children who are 10 years of age or younger must complete a competency hearing in order to qualify to testify in trial.

A child must be able to communicate that he or she knows the difference between the truth and a lie and understands the consequences of the two.

Interviewer: Susie, what if I said the judge has purple hair? Is that the truth or a lie?
Child: A lie.
Interviewer: Why?
Child: Because his hair is brown.
Interviewer: What happens when a person tells a lie?
Child: They get in trouble 'cuz you're not supposed to lie. Like you might get grounded or spanked or something.

In a competency hearing or even grand jury and preliminary hearings, it must be established that the child has a memory for details and can communicate that information accurately and without assistance. For this reason, the dolls are generally not brought to the hearing. They could be viewed as a "prop" or "crutch" for the child. It is appropriate, however, if the interviewer describes the previous investigative interview in which the child used dolls.

In situations with older children age 8 or older, the dolls may actually help establish competency. For example, in the investigative interview, did the child pick out the doll of the correct sex to represent him or her? If the child was a girl, did she pick out the girl doll? Was the selected doll the correct age (adult vs. child doll)? If there were dolls of different skin colors, did the child pick out the doll of the appropriate race? As stated previously, a word of caution: Do not expect very young children to be able to differentiate race, age, or sex of the dolls.

❑ **The Trial**

On the day you go to court, take along some items that will help pass the time and keep the child occupied. Crayons and paper, a coloring book, a story book, or a simple board game will give the child something to do while waiting to testify and relieve his or her nervousness. Throughout the court process, continually convey a positive, supportive attitude. This will let the child know you believe what he or she is saying and that you know the child can be a good witness.

If the dolls have not been used in your area previously, if they have not been used in your particular judge's courtroom, or if you anticipate a challenge from the defense attorney, there are several preliminary steps to take. Meet with the judge and defense attorney before the trial in a "camera hearing" (outside the presence of the jury). Show the dolls to the judge and defense attorney. Explain that the anatomical dolls (note: not "anatomically correct dolls") are going to be used in the trial for "demonstrative purposes." Explain that, like a map of the intersection used in a traffic accident case, the dolls are a "map of the body." They are a representation, not a replica. Communicate that the dolls are not toys—they are investigative tools, such as anatomical drawings, puppets, manikins. They are simply designed to help facilitate and clarify the witnesses' testimony.

If the judge or defense attorney needs convincing that the dolls are appropriate in the courtroom, explain that they have been used in hundreds of sexual abuse cases since 1976 in all 50 states and numerous foreign countries. Rulings have been made in cases where the dolls have been used, and case law exists (see Chapter 7).

Prior to the trial, take pictures of the dolls. Admit the pictures into evidence rather than the dolls themselves. If the dolls are put into evidence, you will not be able to have access to them for weeks, or, if an appeal is filed, possibly even years. During the trial, the dolls are kept with the other evidence or at the prosecuting attorney's table. If they are kept at the prosecutor's table, have them in their carrying bag, or dressed and on the table. Do not have them lying undressed and visible because that can be distracting. If the dolls are to be used in court, the prosecuting attorney will present them to the child during the child's testimony.

Admit the pictures into evidence rather than the dolls themselves.

The child generally feels more comfortable using the dolls when talking in front of strangers. Having something to hold, look at, and focus on reduces anxiety and self-consciousness. Likewise, testimony using dolls is very graphic for the jury. The words "He put his stick in my hole" do not have nearly the same impact as a child visually demonstrating two dolls having sexual intercourse. With the dolls, there is no doubt in the minds of the judge or the jury as to what transpired.

Be prepared to discuss the verdict with the child. "Guilty" or "not guilty" does not mean the child was believed or not believed. It means enough information was or was not presented to convince the judge or jury in one way or the other. Remind the child that the rules in the court sometimes do not let all the information be given to the judge and the jury.

Not all children can testify in court. Some are simply too young or too emotionally disturbed by what has happened. But most children can do a very good job if given preparation and support.

7

Legal Issues

❏ Common Legal Questions

The proper use of anatomical dolls can be a catalyst for establishing rapport and competency, calming the child, reducing embarrassment in the interview and courtroom, and enhancing clear communication (Freeman & Estrada-Mullaney, 1988; Friedemann & Morgan, 1985). An interviewing protocol is important to ensure the proper and appropriate use of the dolls with children (Boat & Everson, 1988a, 1988b; Freeman & Estrada-Mullaney, 1988; Jampole & Weber, 1987; Walker, 1988; White, Strom, Santilli, & Halpin, 1986). Yet the dolls are not a cure-all, nor do they ensure disclosure or provide a fail-safe method of obtaining the truth (Boat & Everson, 1988a, 1988b).

There are three fundamental legal questions surrounding the use of anatomical dolls:

1. Are the dolls leading and suggestive because they have sexual body parts?

2. Did the interviewer use the dolls in a leading or suggestive manner?

3. Did the interviewer interpret correctly what the child did or did not do with the dolls?

ARE ANATOMICAL DOLLS LEADING AND SUGGESTIVE?

Yates and Terr (1988a, 1988b) debated the empirical reliability of anatomical dolls. Terr believed that the dolls were not a useful interviewing tool because "the anatomically correct dolls make but one request, 'play sex.' " She concluded, therefore, that they are suggestive and directive.

Perhaps we should first look at what we mean by *leading* and *suggestive*. The common usage would suggest that the dolls are out of the norm or status quo, that they imply something sexual, directly or indirectly, or evoke or influence sexual thoughts or behaviors. As discussed in Chapter 1, most anatomical dolls have sexual body parts that are proportionate (Bays, 1990) and therefore have bodies similar to the human body.

Given that the physical structure of the dolls is not proportionately suggestive, the next question may be, What do children *do* when exposed to dolls' genitalia? The dolls' suggestiveness may need to be analyzed in terms of whether the child who sees the dolls is sexually knowledgeable or experienced to begin with, or whether he or she is sexually naive. Many professionals believe that sexual knowledge in a young child is a consequence not of doll-induced fantasy but of prior sexual exposure or experience. The dolls provide an impetus for the interviewer or evaluator to explore, through observation and questioning, the depth and source of the child's sexual knowledge.

> *Sexual knowledge in a young child is not a consequence of doll-induced fantasy.*

Perhaps the focus of the doll-suggestiveness debate should be on the non-abused, sexually uneducated child. If the dolls' genitalia make these children respond the same way as sexually abused children, then this would indeed be a cause for concern. However, the research does not support this notion.

In one study, for instance, eighty 3- and 5-year-old children were individually given an opportunity to play games with a man (Goodman & Aman, 1990). One game, "Simon Says," had the child touch his or her own body and at one point touch the man's knee. One week later, the children were interviewed about the play session. Each child was interviewed in one of three ways: (a) with regular dolls, (b) with anatomical dolls, or (c) with no dolls. The children were asked several things, including a series of three suggestive questions: (a) "He took your clothes off, didn't he?" (b) "How many times did he spank you?" (c) "He kissed you, didn't he?"

The children who had anatomical dolls as props did not make any more errors in their responses than did children with regular dolls or no dolls. Despite an intentionally leading interview, the use of anatomical dolls compared to regular dolls did not heighten the children's suggestibility.

In another study examining a child's free recall versus recall using anatomical dolls as a visual aid, seventy-two 5- and 7-year-olds were asked to describe a medical exam they had had at a doctor's office 1 month earlier (Saywitz, Goodman, Nicholas, & Moan, 1991). The dolls produced twice as much accurate information as was obtained using free recall with no props. There was some reporting error when children were asked closed-ended, yes/no response questions, but that occurred even when the children were not referring to the dolls' genitalia. The children also showed a great deal of resistance to directed, leading, sexual-abuse-related questions.

Both of these studies do not support that sexually explicit dolls create fantasy, or distort reality and memory in children.

If anatomical dolls are suggestive and sexually stimulating as critics claim, one would find a high frequency of sexually explicit behaviors and play with the dolls. Over 200 presumably nonabused children, ages 2 to 5, from various socioeconomic backgrounds were videotaped exploring the dolls (Everson & Boat, 1990). Touching and exploration were common in over 50% of the cases whether or not an adult was present. However, vaginal, oral, and anal intercourse, such as the child putting his or her mouth on the doll's genitals or emulating intercourse, occurred in only 6% of the sample.

This small percentage of sexually explicit behavior with the dolls is consistent with the research results in nine other studies where nonabused children were observed with anatomical dolls (August & Forman, 1989; Cohn, 1991; Dawson & Geddie, 1991; Dawson, Vaughn, & Wagner, 1992; Gabriel, 1985; Glaser & Collins, 1989; Jampole & Weber, 1987; Sivan, Schor, Koeppl, & Noble, 1988; White et al., 1986). These studies provide substantial evidence that anatomical dolls do not force young, nonabused, sexually naive children to engage in explicit sexual play. However, as stated earlier, sexually knowledgeable children may find anatomical dolls to be a means to demonstrate their knowledge, not to create new knowledge.

The notion that the anatomical dolls' sexual parts promote fantasy has been debated in the literature and in the media. Some have argued the genitals and body openings (mouth, vagina, anus) suggest a play pattern to children that interviewers misinterpret as evidence of sexual abuse (Gabriel, 1985; Philippus & Koch, 1986; Yates & Terr, 1988a, 1988b). As stated above, however, others have found evidence to the contrary.

DID THE INTERVIEWER USE THE DOLLS IN A LEADING OR SUGGESTIVE MANNER?

The second question, whether the interviewer used leading interviewing techniques, is an issue that often arises in a trial or juvenile court hearing. A directive, suggestive, or leading question is one that suggests its own answer in the question itself, or is designed to obtain specific information. It can also be a question that elicits a yes or no response. One safeguard against an accusation of the interviewer using leading questions is to audio or videotape the interview (Freeman & Estrada-Mullaney, 1988; Walker, 1988) or to have another adult present to document and verify what was said and how it was said. Additionally, all touching should be done by the child, not the adult interviewer, because leading and coercion can also be nonverbal.

Many interviewers do not know how to ask questions using the anatomical dolls, or they may overly rely on the dolls to the exclusion of other communication techniques and nonverbal tools such as drawings or toy telephones. In a study of 119 professionals who used dolls, very few had access to a manual or set of interviewing guidelines, and almost all doll users (86%) endorsed the need for a standard protocol that they could follow when presenting the dolls (Boat &

Everson, 1988a, 1988b). The researchers also found that most interviewers who used dolls had little or no specific training in doll use.

With no standard questions or protocol, interviewers run the risk, often unintentionally, of some suggestive questioning.

Most interviewers who used dolls had little or no specific training in doll use.

Researchers have also tried to analyze how much children are influenced and susceptible to leading questions. They have determined that if subjects find an event understandable and interesting and their memory for it is still strong, then there are no differences between adults and children in suggestibility relating to that event. If a child's memory of the abuse is minimal or fragmented, and if he or she does not have good language skills (so that he or she is oblivious to the subtle implications in the suggestive information), then the child may be immune to the manipulation.

Another form of leading the child might be through the interviewer posing or positioning the dolls, coupled with verbal prompts (e.g., "Is this what happened with you and Daddy?"). As presented in the chapter on how to interview using anatomical dolls, always have the child select and handle the dolls (unless the child directs you to hold the dolls in a specific way).

DID THE INTERVIEWER INTERPRET CORRECTLY WHAT THE CHILD DID OR DID NOT DO WITH THE DOLLS?

The third question is perhaps the most nebulous. How does an interviewer accurately interpret what a child does with the dolls? Anatomical dolls are useful in enabling the examiner to understand the child and form an opinion (Yates & Terr, 1988a, 1988b). Yet is there consensus in that opinion as well as professional standards and guidelines to draw consistent, reliable conclusions? If the dolls are to be used as a demonstration aid in the interview (Everson & Boat, 1994), then there is no need to "interpret" anything. The child may simply be communicating, "This is what happened to me."

Several studies have concluded that sexually abused children do act differently with the dolls than children who have not been abused

(Jampole & Weber, 1987; White et al., 1986). Although still being debated, these results are slowly beginning to provide a foundation for the professional community (police, social workers, child protective service workers) in their work interpreting and validating children's behaviors.

The researchers studied the ability of interviewers who were unaware of children's abuse histories in order to discriminate between the behavior of both abused and nonabused children with anatomical dolls. Both White et al. (1986) and Jampole and Weber (1987) found that interviewers were able to determine significant differences in the way sexually abused and nonabused children behaved with the dolls. Interviewers were also more prone to false negatives than false positives (White et al., 1986)—that is, they were more likely to classify an allegedly abused child as nonabused than vice versa. One study showed that nine out of 10 sexually abused children demonstrated sexual behaviors with anatomical dolls. In that same study, eight out of 10 nonabused children did not demonstrate any sexual behavior with the dolls (Jampole & Weber, 1987). Even though the numbers are high, it is important to note two out of the 10 did show sexualized behaviors. Therefore abused and nonabused children cannot be reliably differentiated solely on their behaviors with the dolls. Between 1985 and 1994, 12 studies were conducted on interpreting children's reactions to anatomical dolls (Everson & Boat, 1994). These studies offer substantial evidence that (a) among normal, presumably nonabused young children, touching and exploration of the genitals of the dolls is fairly common, but enactments of sexual intercourse are relatively rare; and (b) sexually abused young children are more likely than their nonabused peers to play and interact with the dolls in sexual ways.

❏ Case Law Regarding Doll Use

There is legal precedent concerning the admissibility of evidence obtained from using anatomical dolls. In the U.S. Appellate Court, 9th Circuit case of *U.S. v. Gillespie* (87-5067), the appellate decision declared that the expert testimony using anatomical dolls was subject to the "Frye test." This is based on the 1923 Supreme Court case of *Frye v. U.S.*, which held that evidence is admissible only if it has been generally accepted in the scientific community as being reliable. Therefore there is no decision on whether the dolls *should* be used in a court of law, but only that the dolls must be qualified under the Frye test, meaning that professionals in the field use them as an accepted, reliable interviewing assessment tool.

Two other appellate court cases ruled that experts were permitted to offer how the child used the dolls as circumstantial evidence of abuse but could not offer an opinion as to whether the use of dolls indicated abuse (Bulkley, 1988). Therefore the clinician cannot conclude a child was abused, but rather that the child believed the defendant committed sexual abuse.

There is a great deal of debate over children's ability to recall accurately and whether their memories are more fragmented than adults'. Hence their behaviors with the dolls are not necessarily based on accurate, historical recollections. However, reviews of research in the area of children's memory show that children are able to retain information nearly as accurately as adults but may be less able to recall or reenact events using free association and open-ended questions, are more likely to improve their descriptions of events when asked specific questions using inanimate props such as dolls (particularly children ages 2½ to 5½ years), are not likely to create fantasy responses to toy props, are no more prone to lying than adults are, are no more likely to fabricate complex allegations than adults are, and are less capable than adults of recalling past events without prompting if they are younger than 9 years old. With appropriate cues and questioning, children as young as 3 years can recall past events.

The use of anatomical dolls as a demonstration aid to testimony in court is not uncommon. In fact, it is so commonplace that it is often mentioned without issue in appellate cases. Yet the dolls have not gone unchallenged in both criminal and civil litigations.

Related to the professional's observation of the child's behavior with the dolls is the legal concern regarding the hearsay rule. Lower court decisions, even when reversed on other grounds, generally uphold the use of anatomical dolls at trial and pretrial. However, hearsay rules and exceptions govern admissibility of a victim's statements made to psychologists, psychiatrists, social workers, or police officers who conduct interviews using anatomically detailed dolls.

"Hearsay" becomes an issue when the victim is found incompetent to testify. Failure to prove the victim's incompetence may result in the exclusion of hearsay. Additionally, witness/victim competence and admission of demonstrative evidence are not necessarily interdependent. The admissibility of demonstrative evidence depends only upon whether it is, in the court's discretion, of aid to the trier of fact. In one case, for example, the witness's ability to demonstrate what happened to her using dolls was evidence to the court of her competence to testify, although when a child victim is competent to testify, use of anatomical dolls is generally upheld as an aid to testimony.

Finding a young victim incompetent to testify may trigger application of hearsay exceptions, thus allowing admission of testimony of observed victim behavior or statements. But people with testimony about a victim's conduct or statements may be admitted, in any event, for more narrow purposes. Some courts have upheld testimony about observed nonverbal behavior while alleged victims were using anatomical dolls. These cases typically allow testimony to show whether a particular person was the abuser. Lack of adequate foundation by the proffering party may prevent testimony about even nonverbal conduct as admissible hearsay.

Additionally, courts have admitted hearsay under state law equivalents of Federal Rules of Evidence 803(1), 803(2), 803(4), and 803(24). The hearsay exceptions allow testimony about a child's conduct when using the dolls, provided that the circumstances fall within an exception to the rule or the residuary section, which may be construed narrowly.

The reported cases imply that doll use per se is not a viable issue on appeal. Although the advent of anatomical dolls in criminal law is relatively recent, the use of demonstrative aids, in general, has longstanding acceptance with courtroom testimony. The propriety of using anatomical dolls is measured by whether its admission will assist the trier of fact in understanding a witness's testimony, consistent with the normal rule for demonstrative aids. No known case has overruled the use of anatomical dolls altogether. Instead, the dolls are mentioned in collateral issues involving grounds for reversal.

The association of doll use with reversal might be one reason for their sometimes controversial use. Alternatively, the recent advent of these dolls might explain the limited number of challenges on appeal, or the small number of cases may be the result of prosecutorial discretion. Prosecutors may be reluctant to expend trial resources on a child victim who is unable to testify without the use of demonstrative aids like anatomical dolls. Witness competency also figures heavily in deciding to go forward with a case. Generally, young children (between 1 and 3 years of age) are considered ineffective witnesses. Ironically, the value of anatomical dolls as a demonstrative aid is lost to the youngest victims. Young victim testimony might benefit most from doll use in terms of allowing victims to be understood. Where testimony about a victim's nonverbal conduct is allowed, it seems logical to likewise allow nonverbal victim testimony by demonstration.

Doll use per se is not a viable issue on appeal.

Beyond capacity to testify, practitioners have expressed concern about further psychological trauma to the victim from court testimony. These concerns have given rise to a battery of suggested legislative reforms. But authority is divided on the propriety of hearsay reforms, videotaping testimony, and whether other alternatives to in-court child victim testimony actually are any less traumatic for the victim.

The viability of anatomical dolls as demonstrative aids is not really disputable under current law. The lower and appellate court decisions regarding doll use in investigation and prosecution uphold their use and help maintain their acceptance in the legal community.

It is impossible to cover every legal issue an interviewer might encounter using anatomical dolls. It is, however, important to know that an interviewer's words, tools, and actions with alleged child victims may become the focus of intense scrutiny and criticism if the case goes to court or a juvenile hearing. Defense attorneys may assert that the interviewer's methods and techniques lead to false disclosures and incorrect clinical diagnoses of abuse. Therefore it is essential for interviewers to meet with their local prosecutors to discuss protocol with the dolls and receive training on current accepted doll usage.

8

Training Exercises

The best way to get acquainted with the dolls is to practice using them in interviews. The following two exercises should help you feel more comfortable and confident in an interview.

❑ Exercise 1: Role Playing

Break into groups of two people. Assign one person to be the "interviewer" and the other person to be the "child." Give each person the information listed below that corresponds to his or her role. (Putting the information on cards works well.) Do not let the "interviewer" see what is on the "child's" card and vice versa. The object in this role-playing exercise is for the "interviewer" (police officer or caseworker) to get all the information on the "child's" card by using the dolls and appropriate nonleading questions.

With each new role-play situation, have the "interviewer" and the "child" switch roles. Take about 15 to 20 minutes for each situation.

At the end of the exercise, take a few minutes to critique each other and debrief the experience. Take care to explore the experience from the perspective of both the interviewer and the child.

Situation 1

Interviewer: You just received a telephone call from a grandmother concerned about Vicki, her 5-year-old granddaughter. Vicki spent the weekend with her and, while playing with the neighbor kids, kept trying to pull down their pants. She also suggested to the other kids that they "lick each other's bottoms." The grandmother noticed that Vicki masturbated often and was not concerned about going to a private place to do so. You have set up a time to talk to Vicki at the day care center.

Child: You are a 5-year-old who lives with your mother and her girlfriend. You are an only child. Both your mother and her girlfriend have boyfriends who sometimes babysit you. Your mother's boyfriend is nice to you. The girlfriend's boyfriend is also nice, but sometimes he plays some funny games. The games are always to be kept a secret. At first they were a little scary because he made you pull down your pants and lie on the couch and then he licked your bottom. After awhile, you realized it felt good to touch your bottom like he did, so you touch yourself whenever you want to. You never told your mom because it was supposed to be a secret. You did notice that it seemed to bother your grandmother, with whom you stayed overnight this past weekend. You are at the day care center coloring a picture when a police officer/case worker comes up to you to talk. You don't know why and are a little frightened.

Situation 2

Interviewer: You are called to a local junior high school by a counselor. She tells you she has been concerned about an eighth-grade girl, Jennifer, for quite some time.

There has never been anything specific until today. Another girl, Gayle, told the counselor that last weekend when she spent the night at Jennifer's house, Jennifer's father tried to get both girls to undress for him. Jennifer was able to talk her father out of this and promised him "something special" later. Jennifer does not know you are coming to the school to talk to her nor that Gayle disclosed this information to the counselor.

Child: You are a 14-year-old girl named Jennifer. You have been sexually involved with your natural father since the second grade. It started with him fondling you. When you were in the fourth grade he asked you to start "jacking him off" and to suck on his penis. Finally, when you reached age 12 he said you needed to learn about "real sex" and started having vaginal intercourse with you. He always buys you treats like records, make-up, and clothes. You decided recently that you are tired of all this. When you told your father, he laughed and said he only does this for your own good so that you don't have to learn about sex on the streets. This weekend, he asked both you and your friend Gayle to undress for him. Gayle was scared, so you promised to stay home with him the next night. You are afraid to tell your mom about this because she seems jealous of the special treats and special attention you get. You have just gotten called out of science class to report to the counselor's office. You have no idea why.

Situation 3

Interviewer: You received a call from Mrs. Furby stating she knew of an 8-year-old child who was being sexually abused and forced to masturbate an older man named "John." You got the child's name, Kyle, but that is just about it. You have made an appointment through Kyle's mom and dad to meet Kyle at school.

Child: You are an 8-year-old boy named Kyle. Uncle John babysits you two to three times a month whenever your mom and dad go to their bowling league games. Uncle John always kisses you and puts his tongue inside your mouth. Sometimes he'll have you sit on his lap and pull his "thing" out of his pants because he says it itches. You have told your mom that you don't like to kiss or be around Uncle John, but all she says is, "Be nice to him, he's part of the family." You told your best friend's mom, Mrs. Furby, about it yesterday. Now someone is coming to your school to talk to you. You think it might have something to do with this, but you are afraid to say anything because you might get in trouble.

Situation 4

Interviewer: A teacher from a local school for the emotionally/mentally handicapped called to report that a 14-year-old mentally retarded student was raped Saturday. The teacher is bringing the girl to your office today.

Child: You are a 14-year-old girl and attend a school for the emotionally/mentally retarded. Physically, you have developed into adulthood. You don't understand why men now say things to you about your breasts, nor why last Saturday that one man gave you a ride from downtown and kept touching your breasts. He was really funny. He even put his "wienie" in your "bottom" (where you go number 1, not number 2). You told your teacher about him Monday morning. You could remember it was a small blue "bug" car with dice in the mirror and that he was in his 20s and white. You're really excited because a police officer is going to talk to you at City Hall about something.

❏ **Exercise 2: Leading Versus Nonleading Questions**

In an interview with a child, the following questions and actions may be interpreted as being "leading." A defense attorney could accuse an interviewer of directing the child to give a certain answer just by the way the question was phrased. The goal of this exercise is to develop good interviewing questions by rephrasing the leading questions listed below.

Leading Questions

1. Did Mr. Smith threaten you?
2. Did you feel frightened?
3. Had your mom been drinking?
4. If you tell me what your dad "did" to you when you were camping, I'll let you have some ice cream.
5. Is that when he had sex with you?
6. Did he put his hand down your pants?

Sample Alternative Questions

1. What did Mr. Smith do?
2. How did you feel?
3. What was your mom doing before this?
4. Let's talk about what happened last Tuesday, when you and your dad went camping.
5. What happened next?
6. What was he doing? (or) What was he doing with his hands?

9

Review Checklist:
Interviewing Dos and Don'ts

❏ **Preinterview Preparation**

_____ 1. Interview the complainant first, face to face if possible, not over the telephone. He or she may provide information on how the child might respond and be an important link between you and the young victim.

_____ 2. Interview the child victim immediately.

  a. Choose the interview setting (minimal disruption, comfortable, and free from parental pressure).

  b. Carefully decide whether you will videotape or record the interview or just take notes.

  c. Interview the child by him or herself if possible.

  d. Multiple interviews are OK (two or three interviews may be enough) by the same interviewer or team.

  e. Try not to wear a uniform to interview. The offender has probably told the child he or she will get into trouble if he or she "tells," so the child will be afraid to talk to police.

    f. Do not interview a child during his or her normal nap time.

❑ The Interview

    ____ 1. Establishing Rapport

        a. Introduce yourself and establish a rapport. Get on the child's level (i.e., down on the floor). Talk about school, play games, color. Keep extra clothes at work so you won't mind getting dirty. Talk to the child about your job and what you do.

        b. Ask child if he or she knows why you are there to talk. Give ample time for the child to disclose. If the child says nothing, say that "someone is concerned about you" or state specifically what the child told the complainant. Talking on play telephones may also facilitate discussion.

        c. Tell the child that you talk to a lot of kids and that he or she is not alone. "Don't worry. What you say won't surprise or shock me or make me mad at you."

        d. Use the child's phrases like "Trouble at home? What kind of trouble?" Always use the child's words: "You say he touched your peanuts?"

        e. Create the opportunity to acknowledge that the child may be upset or afraid that you are there. Be reassuring. "I know this must be difficult for you, but I am here to listen and to help you."

        f. Ask about the first time something happened. It is less threatening than to ask about the most recent incident. This will help show logical progression.

        g. Do not use leading questions. Say, "What happened next?" not "Did he pull down your pants?" Leading questions generally elicit yes or no answers.

        h. It may be helpful to draw a diagram of the room or location where the abuse occurred. When the dolls are used in an interview, allow the child to use the entire room to recreate the incident location.

        i. To establish the element of secrecy, even if the child said he or she never told anyone about the abuse, ask, "What did your mom say about this?" "Your teacher?" "Aunt Betty?" The child may state, "I never told them, it was a secret." This also helps establish what enticement was used by the offender.

        j. Do not touch the child unless he or she touches you first and the touching is appropriate.

_____ 2. Establishing Incident Details

    a. Introduce the dolls if the child has given you some indication that the incident was sexual and he or she needs help describing details.

    b. State that you have some dolls that are special dolls because they help you in talking to children. Let the child know the dolls have all body parts. That way, the child sees you as more "human" because you have dolls, and the child will understand that he or she cannot keep the dolls at the end of the interview.

    c. Introduce the dolls with or without clothes, depending upon (1) the interviewer's individual preference and comfort level, and (2) whether the clothes were an important part of the story.

    d. Do a body parts inventory with the child, starting with the public parts such as the arm or leg, and ask, "What is this?" Then alternate asking about the private parts of the body. Do not correct the child; use his or her terms.

    e. Have the child pick a doll to represent him or her. Do not use the word *pretend* or hand the doll to the child. If the child picks the doll of the right sex and age, this may be helpful information that can be used in a competency hearing later on.

    f. Have a child pick a doll to represent the abuser. By this time, you probably have a name to say—"Uncle John" or "Fred Smith."

    g. It is not unusual for a child to put fingers in the doll's body openings or put one doll's penis into the other doll's vagina. This in and of itself may not indicate sexual abuse.

    h. Always underreact. A simple "Uh-huh" and a nod are generally effective.

    i. Although it may be tempting, do not bribe the child to talk (e.g., offering cookies).

    j. If you suspect the child is lying, do not be accusatory. Say, "Tell me about that again, only this time, tell me only the part that is true, OK?"

    k. Using "active feedback" or "reflection," replay the victim's statements.

_____ 3. Validating the Child's Story

    a. Parents are generally not validators unless they confess the abuse, they witnessed the abuse, or they confirm that the child made prior disclosures to them.

    b. Multiple incidents—did the offender have access to the child over a period of time? If so, there is good likelihood of multiple incidents.

    c. Progression of sexual activity—did it begin with touching and become more intimate?

    d. Child should be able to give explicit details about the sex act.

    e. Surrounding details—child should be able to recite details about what else was occurring at the time of the incidents (e.g., it was Aunt Marge's birthday, Doug got a new dog, Dennis came to visit).

    f. You can often tell if a child has been coached by the way he or she repeats statements or uses big words. If the sex act was sudden or violent, the child may have difficulty with recall in d and e above.

____ 4. End of the Interview

    a. Praise the child for talking to you. Once again, emphasize that the blame lies with the offender and not with the child.

    b. Explain what the next step will be for the child. It is best not to discuss what will happen 6 months from now unless the child brings it up.

    c. Review any notes you have taken with the child to make sure you were accurate.

    d. End the interview with casual talk (use rapport-building information) and by asking the child if she or he has any questions. Do not offer bribes, such as food. Make the child feel that the interview was a positive experience. Help the child identify a safe person he or she can contact.

____ 5. Report Writing

    a. In your written report, give general information of what occurred. Details, which could later change, may be used detrimentally in court by the defense (prior inconsistent statements). The prosecutor can use these details in pretrial conferences, if they are necessary for the trial.

❏ Pretrial Preparation

____ 1. Show the child the courtroom. Explain who sits where and their purpose.

____ 2. Practice a brief witness interview/cross-examination with the prosecutor in the courtroom and using the dolls. Practice is extremely important.

____ 3. Practice with the prosecutor presenting the case at least once.

_____ 4. Talk about what to wear, general courtroom "rules" such as not chewing gum, etc.

_____ 5. Bring coloring books or other activities to occupy children as they wait to be called to testify.

_____ 6. Ask the child if he or she would like a support person to sit with him or her in the courtroom. If so, pick a person who will not be a witness. Have the person come to the courtroom practice sessions and sit where he or she will sit during the trial.

10

Future Issues and Trends

The use of anatomical dolls is more commonplace today throughout the United States, Canada, and many foreign countries than it was 5 or 10 years ago. Additionally, in the next few years, there will be an increase in their use and acceptance inside and outside the United States as legal and social systems worldwide struggle with an increase in child sexual abuse cases. This will only occur, however, if they are used appropriately and correctly.

There is also a trend to get away from using homemade/handmade anatomical dolls. In the early years of doll use, professionals were seeking low-cost alternatives, often having "someone in the office" just sew some dolls and add the sexual parts. However, as discussed in Chapter 1, the legal system, particularly the defense bar, has challenged the accuracy, proportionality, and suggestiveness of many homemade dolls. There are several "professional" anatomical doll companies who are aware of these legal challenges. Some dolls even come with condoms, sanitary napkins, tampons, and, for babies, umbilical cords. The dolls have become more expensive but more detailed, durable, and versatile as well.

Another trend is having specially equipped and "child-friendly" interview rooms. As more child victims become involved in our legal and social system, the need to handle these cases becomes more critical. Many areas are expanding this idea and developing child assessment centers where a specialized, trained team of experts handles these cases. They have social, legal, and medical staff to respond to alleged abuse victims. Additionally, assessment centers have various interview tools available, such as dolls, and have staff who know how to use them.

A growing concern is in the area of training for child abuse interviewers. As more government and private social service agencies face fiscal constraints, cutbacks become necessary. Often one of the first areas to be eliminated is professional staff training. Because of this trend, and because of the high turnover of staff in stressful occupations such as social service and law enforcement, many interviewers will go untrained or undertrained. This is unfortunate for the staff, who need to keep current on case law, research, and interview techniques and practices. It is also unfortunate for victims, whose cases may not be handled properly.

Perhaps the most distressing trend in the use of anatomical dolls is the actions by some police, prosecutors, and child protective service offices to stop using the dolls altogether. This has partially been due to negative publicity on a few cases where dolls were used. The problems in these cases were how the dolls were used in interviews, not the dolls themselves. Some highly publicized cases in the media have focused on these "suggestive dolls" and how they have "destroyed cases." As discussed in the chapter on legal issues, the interviewer may have simply used the dolls inappropriately.

Without a doubt, there has been a backlash in response to the high number of child sexual cases coming before the authorities. As with any social issue that is emotionally charged and affects people's rights, there is bound to be disbelief and questioning. Some argue that the tension of a point-counterpoint is a necessary social phenomenon and is important to keep us all thinking critically and behaving professionally. The pendulum will swing back and forth a few times before settling at a middle ground where children and adults are respected and heard. It is here that both victims' and offenders' rights are acknowledged and it is hoped that justice will prevail.

Groups and organizations have formed to challenge the credibility of counselors who work with sexual abuse victims.

As part of this backlash, groups and organizations have formed to challenge the credibility of counselors who work with sexual abuse victims. They suggest that counselors read too much into their clients' problems and convince them, through repeated questioning or prior assumptions, that these problems stem from having been sexually abused when they were young. The concept of the False Memory Syndrome (FMS) developed from this concern, and attempts to provide an explanation for why there has been an increase in reported abuse cases. Long-term memory issues began to surface when the statute of limitations was lifted on people suing years later for early abuse that had been repressed. The FMS movement will no doubt continue to challenge the practice of professionals working with victims in the areas of sexual abuse and mental health.

Appendix 1

Glossary:
Correct Terms and
Slang for Sexual Parts of the Body

Many times children describe sexual acts using words that are unfamiliar to the adult interviewer. The terms listed below are designed to help bridge the communication gap that might exist between interviewer and child. Remember not to put words in the child's mouth but rather to get clarification and definition of the child's terms, such as through demonstrating with an anatomical doll.

Anus: The opening in the buttocks from which a bowel movement comes. The posterior opening of the digestive tract. Slang: asshole, butthole, airhole.

Breasts: Glands on the chest of a person, located between the neck and abdomen. Slang: boobs, tits, knockers, hooters, headlights.

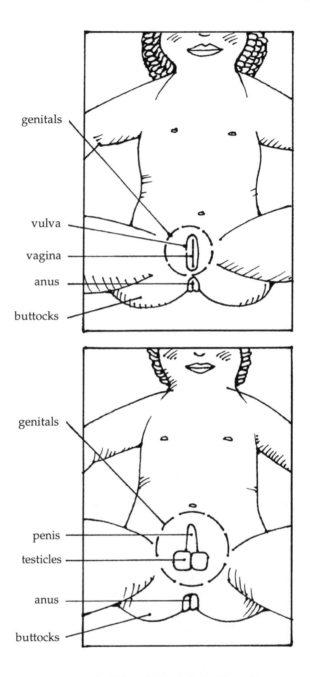

Figure A.1. Anatomical Dolls With Labeled Body Parts

Buttocks: The rear or posterior part of a person's anatomy. Slang: ass, butt, bottom, buns, tush, bum, cheek, rear, seat.

Genitals: The reproductive organs (generally external) on a male or female. Slang: privates, private parts, personal area, bottom.

Penis: The male sexual organ used in sexual intercourse and from which a male urinates. Slang: wienie, cock, johnson, peanuts, snake, thing, wagger, whacker, dick, prick, old fella, peter, dong, rod.

Sexual Intercourse (coitus): The act of putting the male's penis into the female's vagina, often followed by ejaculation. Slang: fucking, screwing, banging, doing it, knocking up, getting some, making love, making babies, humping, piece.

Sodomy: Anal intercourse or oral sex (mouth to genitals). Slang: go down, blow job.

Sperm: A male reproductive cell; spermatozoon. Found in seminal fluid in ejaculation from the penis. Slang: glue, wad, seeds.

Testicles: The two male genital glands, located behind the penis, which produce sperm. Slang: balls, nuts, bag, sack.

Vagina: An opening leading from the uterus to the vulva in a female's genital area. Slang: hole, beaver, cherry (hymen).

Vulva: External female genitalia. Slang: lips, cunt, pussy, jewels.

Appendix 2

Research Review and Annotated Bibliography

The following annotated bibliography consists of research articles on interviewing techniques with child sexual abuse victims. The intent is to provide an overview of the research in the field of interviewing and in particular the use of anatomical dolls, and does not purport to be a comprehensive review of the literature.

August, R. L., & Forman, B. D. (1989). A comparison of sexually abused and non-sexually abused children's behavioral responses to anatomically correct dolls. *Child Psychiatry and Human Development, 20*(1), 39-47.

A research study involving 32 girls, ages 5 through 7, compared children's responses to anatomical dolls. Half of the girls were from treatment or evaluation programs for sexually abused children; the other half were from a "nonabused" control group. The girls were observed playing alone with the dolls and talking about the dolls with a clinician later. The results support the contention that sexually abused children have a different approach to and interaction with the dolls than do nonabused children. The abused children often avoided the doll when an adult was present yet demonstrated more sexual behavior while alone with the doll.

Bays, J. (1990). Are the genitalia of anatomical dolls distorted? *Child Abuse & Neglect, 14*, 171-175.

    This study was undertaken in response to criticisms that the genitalia of anatomical dolls are disproportionate compared to real-life human anatomy. This overemphasis of sexual parts has been perceived as suggestive and misleading to a child when dolls are used in an interview. The results from comparing 17 dolls indicated that the dolls' genitalia were, in fact, appropriately proportioned to the body. The study was conducted only on adult anatomical dolls. However, Bays also offers guidelines for juvenile doll genitalia.

Boat, B. W., & Everson, M. D. (1988). Interviewing young children with anatomical dolls. *Child Welfare, 67*, 337-352.

    This article is a comprehensive look at guidelines for interviewing children under the age of 5 for sexual abuse. It is similar to their earlier booklet of guidelines (see below). It cautions interviewers to obtain adequate training on how to use anatomical dolls and to possess knowledge on child development in order to accurately interpret a child's response. Boat and Everson make suggestions on information the interviewer should know about the child beforehand, the interview setting, and methods of documenting the interview. The interview protocol should focus attention on the child's sexual knowledge and experience in a nondirective manner. Before the interview escalates to questions about the alleged abuse, the interviewer should develop rapport and assess the child's developmental level through questions and play. Ending the interview should leave the child comfortable with having shared possibly difficult and fear-producing information.

Boat, B. W., & Everson, M. D. (1986). *Using anatomical dolls: Guidelines for interviewing young children in sexual abuse investigations.* Chapel Hill: University of North Carolina, Department of Psychiatry, 113-129.

    Guidelines are essential when using dolls to interview young sexual abuse victims. This booklet gives suggestions for the qualities to look for in dolls, such as size, body materials and construction, expression, clothing, sexual features, race, and the number of dolls to use.
    The interview process is broken down into steps corresponding with the three protocol goals: focus the child's attention on sexual issues and experience in a nondirective manner; provide a safe and accepting atmosphere for the child; and provide encouragement and reassurance for the child to overcome reluctance to disclose the abuse. The first step is to build rapport and assess the child's understanding of key concepts. When the dolls are introduced, the interviewer should take a body parts and functions inventory with the child. The child's names for parts or func-

tions should be used throughout the interview. The interview should escalate from a general discussion of times when abuse most likely occurred (e.g., bath time) to the critical event and individuals involved. Questions should be open-ended to avoid being leading. Questions can be asked even during times of play. The interviewer should remain casual and patient and underreact to anything the child says. If the subtle and indirect approach is not productive, the interviewer can ask about sexual abuse in general terms. Escalating beyond this may be leading and suggestive and may not be admissible in court. However, if strong evidence exists, for the safety of the child you may risk direct questions about specific individuals. The last stages of the interview process should focus on the child's specific fears and anxieties. Three appendices include a listing of doll manufacturers, developmental considerations, and criticism of dolls.

Boat, B. W., & Everson, M. D. (1988). Use of anatomical dolls among professionals in sexual abuse evaluations. *Child Abuse & Neglect*, 12, 171-179.

Law enforcement officers, child protection workers, mental health practitioners, and physicians were surveyed to determine their use of anatomical dolls and how they evaluated children's responses. The results indicated that most had little specific training in using the dolls, yet the use of anatomical dolls is increasing. There was also variation among the types of doll features the respondents used. Fewer law enforcement officers considered the child's verbal statements of abuse as convincing evidence. Most of the professional groups believed that sexual demonstrations with the dolls by the children were more convincing if verbal descriptions were added. There was no consensus among the professionals on what behavior was considered normal curiosity or play by the child with the doll. The researchers contend that training in general on the use of the dolls as well as in child development should be a prerequisite for working with young victims of sexual abuse.

Britton, H. L., & O'Keefe, M. A. (1991). Use of nonanatomical dolls in the sexual abuse interview. *Child Abuse & Neglect*, 15, 567-573.

This study addresses the criticism that anatomical dolls are "sexually suggestive" by testing the hypothesis that children who are referred for medical evaluation due to suspected sexual abuse will demonstrate sexual behavior with nonanatomical dolls as frequently as with anatomical dolls. The same researcher interviewed 136 children over a 2-year period. Anatomically detailed dolls were used the first year and nonanatomical dolls the second year. The results of the study supported the hypothesis that the children used the nonanatomical dolls to describe or demonstrate sexual events as frequently as they used the anatomical dolls. The researchers concluded that the use of dolls, whether anatomical or not, is valuable to interviewing young children for sexual abuse because they aid a child in expressing him or herself.

Cohn, D. S. (1991). Anatomical doll play of preschoolers referred for sexual abuse and those not referred. *Child Abuse & Neglect, 15,* 455-466.

This study identified different reactions to anatomical dolls between preschool-age children referred to a hospital clinic for sexual abuse and a "nonabused" control group not referred to the hospital. The children played in a specially prepared room under four conditions. They were observed by two trained coders. The results indicated that the referred children were not more uncomfortable than the control group; neither did they exhibit more aggressive behavior. The two groups were about equally curious about the dolls; thus the researchers concluded that sexual abuse could not be determined solely on the basis of play with the anatomical doll.

Everson, M. D., & Boat, B. W. (1994). Putting anatomical doll controversy in perspective: An examination of the major uses and criticisms of the dolls in child sexual abuse evaluations. *Child Abuse & Neglect, 18*(2).

Through an extensive review of guidelines and protocols on the use of anatomical dolls in sexual abuse evaluations, seven functional uses of the dolls were identified: Comforter, Icebreaker, Anatomical Model, Demonstration Aid, Memory Stimulus, Diagnostic Screen, and Diagnostic Test. These functional uses are discussed in light of several criticisms that have been raised about the use of anatomical dolls in sexual abuse evaluations. The relevance of these criticisms is shown to vary greatly by doll use. As a result, the authors argue that any critique of anatomical dolls must consider the specific function the dolls serve in the evaluation. Although there seem to be widespread perceptions in both lay and professional circles that young children's behavior with the dolls is commonly used to make definitive diagnoses of sexual abuse (Diagnostic Test use), such a use of the dolls was not endorsed by any of the guidelines reviewed and is open to significant criticism. The most common criticism of the dolls, that they are overly suggestive to young, sexually naive children, is not supported by available research. Finally, the continued, informed use of anatomical dolls in sexual abuse evaluations of young children is strongly supported.

Everson, M. D., & Boat, B. W. (1990). Sexualized doll play among young children: Implications for the use of anatomical dolls in sexual abuse evaluations. *Journal of the American Academy of Child and Adolescent Psychiatry, 29*(5), 736-742.

This article begins with an assessment of seven previous studies dealing with explicit sexualized play with anatomical dolls by young children. The study undertaken for this article was to assess these behaviors in a group of nonreferred, nonsuspected children and to note the differences by the child's age, gender, race, and socioeconomic status, and the gender of the interviewer. Two hundred and thirty-three children between the ages of 2 and 5 were used. A 30-minute structured interview with the dolls was conducted with each child. The results of the study suggest that explicit sexualized doll play is not a common occurrence. Only 6% of the children in this study demonstrated this behavior. The behaviors varied in accordance with the various characteristics. The researchers conclude that the dolls are valuable as a communication aid for young children and for differentiating between casual and explicit knowledge of sexual mechanics.

Everson, M. D., Meyers, J.E.B., & White, S. (1993). *Suggested guidelines for use of anatomical dolls during investigations or evaluations of suspected child abuse.* Unpublished manuscript, American Professional Society on the Abuse of Children.

The guidelines offered are for investigative and diagnostic interviews of children by child protection services and law enforcement professionals. The purpose of the guidelines is to provide information on doll use as an adjunct to the questioning process. Seven functions of dolls in investigations and evaluations are identified: Comforter, Icebreaker, Anatomical Model, Demonstration Aid, Memory Stimulus, Diagnostic Screen, and Diagnostic Test. Diagnostic testing with dolls, however, is not an accepted practice. The article discusses where empirical support for doll use exists. For the inexperienced interviewer, more specific guidelines for using dolls in interviews are offered. These include essential features of the dolls, when and how the dolls should be introduced, how to avoid being leading or suggestive, and what to look for in documenting the interview. The appendix offers a list of resources on general interviewing techniques.

Freeman, K. R., & Estrada-Mullaney, T. (1988). Using dolls to interview child victims— Legal concerns and interview procedures. *National Institute of Justice Reports, 207,* 2-6.

This article is aimed at giving both prosecutors and police information on the advantages and disadvantages of, as well as techniques for, anatomical doll use. The advantages are establishing rapport, reducing stress, determining competency, and learning the child's sexual vocabulary. The disadvantages are that the interview techniques are vulnerable to the defense, complicate the case, and allow the possibility of a civil lawsuit. The article gives basic tips and techniques for preinterview considerations, introducing the dolls, learning the child's sexual vocabulary, and determining the case facts. It suggests that interviewers using the dolls should make appropriate selections, know the manual, and plan the interview in advance to avoid rendering the interview inadmissible in court.

Friedemann [Edwards], V., & Morgan, M. (1985). *Interviewing sexual abuse victims using anatomical dolls: The professional's guidebook.* Eugene, OR: Migima Designs.

This was one of the original books on how to use anatomical dolls in investigative interviews. Written by the creators of the anatomical dolls,

it discusses how to select dolls, describes common communication problems in talking with children, and walks the reader step-by-step through
the procedures of an interview: preinterview preparation, establishing
rapport, introducing the dolls, appropriate questioning, interpreting children's actions, legal concerns, and validating the child's information. The
last section includes training exercises for interviewers using dolls, such
as role playing and practice using nonleading questions. The book is 8½ in.
× 5 in., so professionals can easily carry it with them for a reference guide.

Glaser, D., & Collins, C. (1989). The response of young, non-sexually abused children
to anatomically correct dolls. *Journal of Child Psychology and Psychiatry, 30*(4),
547-560.

The article begins with a brief discussion of previous studies on anatomical dolls. This study explored the response of nonabused children to
the dolls, particularly if sexualized play occurred. The children were
allowed to play in a nondirected context in familiar surroundings. The
researchers recorded the emotional and behavioral responses and the
naming of functions. The overall results indicated a positive response of
the children to the dolls. Only five of the 91 children displayed any
sexualized play.

Goodman, G. S., & Aman, C. (1990). Children's use of anatomically detailed dolls to
recount an event. *Child Development, 61*, 1859-1871.

This study was conducted to address the concern that anatomically
detailed dolls lead to false reports of abuse in nonabused children. The
study videotaped 3- and 5-year-olds in a real-life social event with a male
confederate. Children were questioned on the event later with either
anatomical dolls, regular dolls, no dolls but visual cues, or no dolls and
no visual cues. The findings support the view that the dolls do not
contribute to children making false reports of sexual abuse. Although the
3-year-olds were not aided in recall by the props as much as 5-year-olds,
those with props were able to recall a bit more than the children with no
props. The 3-year-olds were also more susceptible to the suggestive or
leading questions.

Gwat-Yong, L., & Inman, A. (1991). The use of anatomical dolls as assessment and
evidentiary tools. *Social Work, 36*, 396-399.

This article reviews the literature on the use of anatomical dolls as well
as implications for their use in social work. The literature subjects include
the use of anatomical dolls, children's credibility, and validity and reliability concerns. Because of those many concerns, the authors warn that
the dolls should still only be used as one of several assessment tools.
Anyone who uses the dolls should undergo training on interview protocol as well as how to interpret and evaluate the responses.

Hewitt, S. K., & Lund, S. J. (1988). *Evaluating the very young child for sexual abuse.* Unpublished manuscript, Midwest Children's Resource Center, Children's Hospital of St. Paul.

This article makes suggestions for interviewing and evaluating sexually abused children between the ages of 18 months and 36 months. Their suggestions to reduce bias include limiting the number of interviews, using open-ended or free recall interview techniques, and using anatomically correct dolls. Their protocol involves four to five interviews to assess the child and establish rapport. Often very young children disclose abuse spontaneously, so objects to stimulate recall, such as anatomical dolls, are suggested. The dolls can also be used for the child's demonstration of abuse. However, the authors are careful to point out that very young children are often not developmentally capable of representational play. Allowing the child to use bodily reenactments may give a clearer picture of abuse in some instances. In order to document the abuse, it must be communicated by the child. The dolls offer one method of nonverbal communication. The article also offers more suggestions for assessing the possibility of parental coaching of allegations.

Jampole, L., & Weber, K. M. (1987). An assessment of the behavior of sexually abused and nonsexually abused children with anatomically correct dolls. *Child Abuse & Neglect, 11,* 187-192.

This study was undertaken to observe possible differences in sexual behavior of sexually and nonsexually abused children while playing with anatomical dolls. The results showed that 90% of the sample of abused children demonstrated sexual behaviors with the dolls, whereas only 20% of the nonsexually abused children did. The researchers concluded that anatomical dolls are useful in sexual abuse investigations.

Kendall-Tackett, K. A. (1992). Professionals' standards of "normal" behavior with anatomical dolls and factors that influence these standards. *Child Abuse & Neglect, 16,* 727-733.

This study attempts to build on previous studies in addressing "normal" behavior standards of a child's response to anatomical dolls among various professionals who work with victims 2 to 9 years of age. Characteristics of the professionals questioned were experience in working with children, experience in working with child victims of sexual abuse, profession, and gender. The majority agreed that overt representation with dolls of sexual behaviors such as oral-genital contact and vaginal intercourse was abnormal for nonabused children. There was disagreement about less obvious behaviors like touching sexual parts of dolls. The rankings depended on the various characteristics of the professionals. Those with the least amount of experience, law enforcement officers, and women were more likely to view the ambiguous behaviors as abnormal.

Kendall-Tackett, K. A., & Watson, M. W. (1992). Use of anatomical dolls by Boston-area professionals. *Child Abuse & Neglect, 16*, 423-428.

This study was conducted as a response to criticisms that anatomical dolls are leading or suggestive to children and that interviewers lacked adequate training and experience to support their assessments of sexual abuse. The study sought to provide information on the characteristics of professionals, situations when doll use is most likely, and the presentation of the dolls to children. The results showed that 96.6% of professionals had received training, 97.3% had at least 1 year of experience with the dolls, and 77.8% followed some standard protocol. The training and protocol were usually derived from multiple sources. The dolls were most often used for children under the age of 10, particularly from 3 to 6 years. The majority of professionals present the dolls fully clothed and have the child undress them to avoid being leading. Also, most present the dolls with regular toys. The dolls are more likely to be used to have the child directly name the body parts and demonstrate what happened than to observe the child playing with the doll. This study contradicts previous findings and calls for further research and sampling in other parts of the country.

Leventhal, J. M., Hamilton, J., Rekedal, S., Tebano-Micci, A., & Eyster, C. (1989). Anatomically correct dolls used in interviews of young children suspected of having been sexually abused. *Pediatrics, 84*(5), 900-906.

This report describes the results of retrospective diagnostic interviews with children under the age of 7 using the anatomical dolls. The information from the doll interviews was classified into a category based on the explicitness of the demonstration. Then the information was compared to noninterview data derived from medical exams, witnesses, confession by perpetrator, or pattern of abuse. In this sample, the researchers found that the dolls were a valuable communication aid for the young children. Thirty-eight percent of the children believed to have been abused would have been missed without the interview using dolls.

Levy, H., Kalinowski, N., Markovic, J., Pittman, M., & Ahart, S. (1991). *Victim-sensitive interviewing in child sexual abuse: A developmental approach to interviewing and consideration of the use of anatomically detailed dolls.* Chicago: Mount Sinai Hospital Medical Center, Department of Pediatrics.

The objective of this monograph, as stated by its authors, is to offer an understanding of when the use of anatomical dolls is appropriate. It provides current research findings and practical training material to allow the reader to make his or her own judgments based on particular instances. It should be used as a supplement to experience or training in child development and/or formal training in interviewing.

Anatomical dolls are only one of a number of facilitative tools. Any interview tool should be suitable to the particular child in order to assist in expressing him or herself. The dolls have been in use for many years; however, no one standardized procedure has been accepted, and there has been minimal consensus among professionals for interpreting children's behaviors with the dolls. The reliability of the dolls is still being debated in both the clinic and the courtroom. Interviewers should be aware of the criticisms that are mentioned by the authors. Despite these criticisms, the authors feel the dolls allow the child to communicate complex situations more easily. In order to make the reader more aware of the controversies over the dolls, the authors include a synopsis of six doll studies, three comparative and three normative. In addition to these, they summarize a research project conducted at Mount Sinai Hospital on the reliability of information obtained through the use of the dolls. Among the findings are a profile of children giving statements regarding abuse, an assessment of demonstrations made with the dolls, a comparison of response assessments by untrained observers and child development specialists, and an examination of interviewers' judgments of child's responsiveness in association with doll utilization. Great emphasis is placed on the interviewer being knowledgeable on child development and on interview techniques. One section offers an overview of child development and an example of an interview training program. Practical guidelines are given for approaching the interview in a sensitive manner. Various phases for conducting the interview are explained and include building rapport, assessing the child's developmental level, integrating the dolls, obtaining incident information, and terminating the interview. Examples of interviews are provided as well as suggestions for handling certain behavioral problems of the child during the interview. The authors also raise questions regarding the interviewer's role that could affect any legal outcome, such as the pros and cons of blind interviews (interviewing the child without obtaining any information about him or her beforehand) and the decision to videotape the interview.

The appendices include a child developmental chart, training resources, assessment recommendations, an overview of interview process, a list of anatomically detailed doll suppliers, and information on available resources on dolls.

MacFarlane, K., & Feldmeth, J. R. (Eds.). (1988). *RESPONSE child sexual abuse: The clinical interview*. New York: Guilford.

This book is a good, practical overview of the clinical interview. It stresses that all interviews should be adapted to the situation and the child's level of development and skills. Besides enhancing the accuracy of information reported by the child, all interviews should have two goals: to make the child comfortable with the interviewer and to avoid causing trauma to the child by the process. In order to increase the accuracy of a child's story, the interviewer should be aware of some common aspects of child sexual abuse as well as barriers to and patterns of disclosure. In approaching the topic of abuse with a child, the interviewer should create a safe and open environment for discussion, encourage the child's disclosure without specific references, and allow the child to disclose in his or her own way and pace without a lot of interruption. By the end of the interview, the child should feel more self-confident and freed from the burden of his or her secret. In responding to the parents, the interviewer should carefully note their reactions to and with the child and aid the parents with reassurance, patience, and counseling. It is also important to take into account the possible legal criticisms of interviewing methods. Only one page of the book is devoted to the use of anatomical dolls and hand puppets. The authors give examples of how the dolls are helpful for interviews with children who have limited verbal ability. The authors state that the dolls have become the "most common aids used in evaluating suspected child abuse cases" and that "it would be a disservice to abused children to see the use of this valuable tool abandoned."

Quinn, K. M., White, S., & Santilli, G. (1989). Influences of an interviewer's behaviors in child sexual abuse investigations. *Bulletin of the American Academy of Psychiatry and Law, 17*(1), 45-52.

Interviewers for child sexual abuse must be aware of how their behavior could influence the child's responses in order to avoid charges of contamination and avoid discrediting the interview. This article addresses both interviewers' behaviors and more technical aspects of the interview. One concern is that if the interviewer holds preconceived impressions, he or she could contaminate the session by implementing techniques that seek to confirm the impressions. Three behavioral aspects are outlined: inappropriate interactional patterns, emotional reactions, and discontinuity of specific behaviors. Interactional levels include assessing the developmental level of the child, touching the child, posture, location, closeness, and materials used in investigation. Emotional reactions may come from the interviewer's tone, language, facial expressions, eye contact, body distance, posture, and gesturing.

Realmuto, G. M., Jensen, J. B., & Wescoe, S. (1990). Specificity and sensitivity of sexually anatomically correct dolls in substantiating abuse: A pilot study. *Journal of the American Academy of Child and Adolescent Psychiatry, 29*(5), 743-746.

The study these authors undertook was to see what scientific merit anatomical dolls have in confirming sexual abuse in young children. Their process involved using "blind" interviewers, both referred and nonreferred control subjects 7 years or younger, a structured interview format, and a defined rating scale. The results of the study found sensitivity to be 33% and specificity 67%. The study's limitations include using a single mental health professional for assessment, a restricted interview protocol, and a small sample size. The researchers concluded that based on these data, anatomical dolls are unsatisfactory as a single stimulus by which to judge abuse; however, they may be valuable as part of a comprehensive psychiatric evaluation in certain subpopulations.

Shamroy, J. A. (1987, March/April). Interviewing the sexually abused child with anatomically correct dolls. *Social Work*, 165-166.

Anatomical dolls, this author contends, are the most important tools an interviewer has for evaluating a young child for sexual abuse. The author gives suggestions for what to look for in anatomical doll features, as well as some general interviewing principles. Two short case examples are included to demonstrate the doll's usefulness in allowing a young child to express him or herself.

Sivan, A. B., Schor, D. P., Koeppl, G. K., & Noble, L. D. (1988). Interaction of normal children with anatomical dolls. *Child Abuse & Neglect*, *12*, 295-304.

One hundred and forty-four nonreferred children were used in this study, which sought empirical information on the play interaction of nonabused children. The children were observed with the dolls under three conditions: with an adult present, without an adult, and with the dolls undressed. The results indicate that nonabused children were not stimulated by the dolls. There were no incidents of aggression or explicit sexual behavior. The researchers conclude that unusual behavior in doll interactions should be taken seriously.

White, S., Strom, G., Santilli, G., & Quinn, K. M. (1987). *Clinical guidelines for interviewing young children with anatomically correct dolls*. Unpublished manuscript, Case Western Reserve University School of Medicine, Cleveland.

These authors provide a structured interview format, to be used with preschool-age children, that is designed to produce reliable, acceptable, and evidentiary data for the judicial system. Suggested interview aids include eight anatomical dolls, which are race appropriate. A "blind" interview, in which the interviewer knows only the child's name and little else about the alleged incident, is suggested. The article describes an interview from start to finish, including greeting the child, handling separation problems, beginning the interview, rapport building, the interviewer's role, the responsiveness of the child, doll presentation and its use through evaluation, developmental issues, and termination. General guidelines are suggested on the number of interviews, how to clarify children's responses, avoiding teaching child body parts and functions, management of interview, reinforcement, and the issue of coercion.

Yates, A., & Terr, L. (1988). Debate forum: Anatomically correct dolls: Should they be used as the basis for expert testimony? *Journal of the American Academy of Child and Adolescent Psychiatry*, *27*, 254-257.

Two professionals debate the issue of whether anatomical dolls should be used as a basis for expert testimony in child sexual abuse cases. Yates defends their use, stating that the dolls are useful in approaching sensitive sexual topics with children being interviewed. Although the dolls have been criticized in the courts, they should continue to be used so techniques can be improved. However, the dolls' importance should not be overstated. Guidelines for doll use, as well as standards or qualifications for examining children, should be established.

The counterpoint to this position is argued by Terr. She writes that the strange appearance of the dolls makes children uncomfortable and suggests only one thing: that they "play sex" with the dolls. The dolls seem to allow interviewers shortcuts in time and training. The dolls also embody a legal conflict between protection of rights and activism.

Yates, A., & Terr, L. (1988). Debate forum issue continued: Anatomically correct dolls: Should they be used as the basis for expert testimony? *Journal of the American Academy of Child and Adolescent Psychiatry, 27*, 387-388.

A California Supreme Court of Appeals decision in 1987 made it difficult to admit evidence from interviews with anatomical dolls. Yates again argues for the use of the dolls. In order to make them more admissible in court, the dolls should continue to be used in order to gain more knowledge and acceptance in the profession. However, she warns, conclusions should not be based on the doll use alone.

Terr argues the negative side. The dolls are a shortcut in evaluation and they are too likely to cause sexual suggestion. She uses a brief interview transcript of a young girl as a case in point. The dolls, she claims, can taint a child's testimony.

Appendix 3

Audiovisual Resources

Act for Kids. (1990). *Interviewing abused children* [Video]. Spokane, WA: Author.

This program examines two types of interviews with children—those conducted by caseworkers and those conducted by law enforcement. Although the style and techniques are similar, the type of information gathered is not.

The professional is walked through the interview steps: (a) preparing for the interview; (b) proper setting for the interview; (c) establishing rapport and assessing the child's development; (d) questioning the child; and (e) concluding the interview.

The video suggests introducing the dolls (referred to as "anatomically correct dolls") if one of three conditions exists: (a) a child has a limited ability to express or verbalize an incident; (b) there is a need to clarify a child's previous statement; or (c) to ease the child's embarrassment by allowing him or her to transfer any anxiety to an inanimate object.

The acting and technical aspects are not those of a highly slick, professional production. However, the information is solid, and this is a good general training video. (24 minutes)

Alberta (Canada) Social Services. (1985). *The child's account: The use of anatomically correct dolls in the investigation of child sexual abuse* [Video]. Charlotte, NC: Kids Rights.

This video is a basic overview of what anatomical dolls are and how they can be used in social service interviews. Although the video may be useful for those just beginning in the field, it may not be comprehensive enough to prepare an interviewer to use the dolls. It is one of the only videos showing male interviewers using dolls. There are some basic problems with the information, however, such as referring to the dolls as "anatomically correct"; making generalizations such as "Children don't lie" (without examining contaminating factors such as parent or offender coaching); displaying inconsistencies, such as saying, "Always interview in a two-person team," but showing only one person; showing examples of interviewers who are very awkward and tense and not good role models; making biblical references, which may not be appropriate for some agencies due to the separation of church and state; using the pronoun she throughout the video, which was distracting when the pictures showed male victims; suggesting that the interviewer refer to dolls as "special friends" (a term often used by offenders when luring or engaging young victims); telling the interviewer to use four dolls ("the same as a family"); and having the interviewer initiate selecting and touching the dolls ("child doll first and perpetrator doll last"). The sound also fades in and out.

Although there are many good suggestions on how to interview (be patient, use open-ended questions, listen, don't be judgmental), some of the information is not based on the most current, empirical data. (24 minutes)

Center for Child Protection, Children's Hospital and Health Center, San Diego. (1988). *Child sexual abuse: Interviewing the young child* [Video]. San Diego: Author.

This videotape encompasses the various stages and components of the forensic interview with the sexually abused child. It addresses the techniques used in interviewing the preschool-age child.

The tape contains excerpts of forensic interviews of young sexual abuse victims conducted at the Center for Child Protection, Children's Hospital and Health Center, San Diego, California. The Center for Child Protection evaluates over 1,100 children annually for suspected sexual abuse and is recognized as a model for evaluating child sexual abuse. (33 minutes)

Center for Child Protection, Children's Hospital and Health Center, San Diego. (1986). *Evaluating developmentally disabled victims of sexual abuse* [Video]. San Diego: Author.

This is a videotape of excerpts of three forensic social work interviews of developmentally disabled victims of sexual abuse conducted at the Center for Child Protection, Children's Hospital and Health Center, San Diego, California.

Children and young adults with developmental disabilities are often not considered credible witnesses by investigating agencies, and consequently many allegations of sexual abuse of the developmentally disabled are not investigated.

This videotape demonstrates to law enforcement, clinicians, and advocates for the developmentally disabled that these victims can give credible histories and that prosecution of the offender and protection of the victim can be achieved. (40 minutes)

Migima Designs. (1985). *Interviewing the young sex crime victim with the aid of dolls* [Audiocassette tape]. Eugene, OR: Author.

An informative cassette tape for training police officers, counselors, child protective service workers, district attorneys, and medical personnel in effective interviewing techniques and courtroom procedures using anatomical dolls. This was one of the early educational audio materials, and although the information is basic, it is still good. Cassette tapes can be listened to in many places, such as cars. They can also have slides added to them to create a low-cost, localized slide-tape training program. (25 minutes)

Migima Designs. (1985). *Sex education: A guide for parents and educators using anatomical dolls* [Audiocassette tape]. Eugene, OR: Author.

This program examines the question, *How much information should I give my child about sex and at what age?* Examples are given of appropriate verbal and nonverbal responses, terminology, and using anatomical dolls. Excellent for parents, PTAs, teacher training, and inservice programs, especially in the areas of health and family life. (22 minutes)

Migima Designs. (1985). *Talking to a child about preventing sexual molestation using anatomical dolls* [Audiocassette tape]. Eugene, OR: Author.

This program examines the problems and symptoms of sexual abuse, how to talk to a child about OK and not OK touches, and what to do if a child is molested. It is a good overview for parents, educators, and social workers and presents the information in a gentle, nonthreatening manner. (20 minutes)

White, S., Quinn, K., Santilli, G., Knell, S., & Wachs, R. (1988). *Child sexual abuse assessment: An investigatory interview* [Video]. Cleveland: Child Guidance Center of Greater Cleveland.

The goal of this video and accompanying study guide is to minimize contamination of interview and children's responses in order to collect data as accurate as possible. *Contamination* means distortion or falsification of sources of a child's memory of alleged events by factors inside or outside the interview. Guidelines and precautions are given to reduce the risk of contamination. Areas focused on in the preinterview procedures are scheduling interviews, parent management, and child management.

The evaluation process includes history from parents and the investigatory interview (environment, interviewer characteristics, free play, and the anatomical doll interview). The video particularly stresses avoiding contamination through interviewer influences and the interviewer's pursuit of an agenda (use of techniques to prompt child to confirm interviewer's assumptions). In other words, it defends the advantages of conducting *blind interviews.* In documenting the interview, tips are given on methods, evaluation reports, and reviewing for contamination. (35 minutes)

White, S., Strom, G., & Santilli, G. (1986). *The young victims of sexual abuse: An interview protocol* [Video]. Cleveland: Child Guidance Center of Greater Cleveland.

This video and the accompanying study guide follow a protocol designed for use with anatomical dolls and toys to determine a child's knowledge of body parts and functions and a child's sexual experiences. This interview should be part of an assessment process that includes a medical examination, parental suspicions, and child statements. Questions and format for interview are given as well as a flow chart. A complete interview conducted by Gail Santilli is shown. (35 minutes)

Appendix 4

Identifying
Symptoms of Sexual Abuse

Often children will not verbalize what is wrong but will convey that they are
troubled by a change in behavior. The following indicators are helpful in
identifying, but may not be isolated to, sexual abuse. Any of these signs could
indicate the child has a problem and needs attention and help.

❑ **Physical Indicators**

- Difficulty in walking, sitting, coordination
- Genital or anal injury (swollen, bleeding)
- Urinating or defecating in clothing (inability to control)
- Venereal disease
- Genital pain and itching
- Change in neatness of appearance

108

- Gaining weight (wearing loose-fitting clothes so as not to draw attention to the body)
- Compulsive masturbation
- Loss of appetite or sudden increase in appetite (and other more serious eating disorders such as anorexia)
- Altered sleep patterns (bedwetting, restlessness, nightmares, fear of sleeping alone, needing a night light, being tired in class)
- Newly acquired bodily complaints, especially stomachaches
- Odor (is not taking care of personal hygiene)

❑ Behavior and Attitude Indicators

- Extreme shifts of emotions/moods
- Fears and phobias especially aimed at one person or location (if a child is afraid to be alone with someone, such as a relative or babysitter, find out why)
- Suddenly turning against someone, such as a parent
- Restlessness
- Acting adultlike, inconsistent with age
- Acting childlike (clinging to adult, sucking thumb)
- Frequent absences from school
- Daydreaming—having learning problems (e.g., drop in grades)
- Irritability, short temper
- Asking questions or having knowledge of terminology inappropriate for child's age
- Expressing affection to adults in inappropriate ways (fondling genitals, French kissing)
- Not willing to undress for PE at school (self-conscious of body)
- Hostility and aggressiveness toward adults or overly trying to please adults
- Afraid to be alone with adults, especially someone the same sex as offender
- Isolation, especially with peers (avoids eye contact, withdrawn)
- Few friends
- Parents don't allow child to stay overnight at friends' houses
- Shying away from being touched
- Having low self-esteem and self-image
- Excessive curiosity about sexual matters (with people and animals)
- Precocious sexual play

Appendix 5

Why Children Don't
Tell Us They Have Been Abused

Most children are sexually abused many times before abuse is ever discovered. There are various reasons why children don't tell us they have a touching problem.

- They are afraid they won't be believed.
- They are afraid of getting into trouble themselves. They feel it is their fault and/or they caused the abuse to occur.
- They may fear threats made by the offender (e.g., break-up of the family, Dad might have to go to jail, fear of rejection by offender and/or family, fear of retaliation).
- They try to protect offender, may love the offender, but don't like the touch.
- Children may not know "how" to tell. They may not know correct words or may describe the situation in vague terms ("Mr. Jones wears funny underpants").

- Children may not know the sexual activity is wrong or even that it is something anyone would want to know about.
- Some children fear peer reaction—being singled out, laughed at, or losing popularity.
- If it was a sexual abuse involving an adult and child of the same sex, they might fear being labeled a homosexual.
- Some older children are embarrassed to discuss sexual issues and intimate details, especially with people of authority (e.g., teachers, police).
- Some children don't know whom to tell.
- Children may not feel there was an "appropriate" time or opportunity to tell.
- They don't want to be labeled a tattletale.
- They have been told that "nice girls/boys" don't use those words that refer to body parts or sexual behavior.

Why do children finally tell someone they are being sexually abused?

- The molestation escalates in frequency or type of behavior and alarms the child.
- The child receives some sexual abuse prevention information and realizes that what has happened to him/her is wrong (that the offender is at fault) and should be reported.
- If the offender has told the child to keep the sexual abuse a secret, sometimes the child may brag or want to share the secret with a best friend, who then reports it.
- The victim's younger brother or sister is now at the age when the victim was first sexually abused, and the victim does not want him or her to be abused as well.
- The child reaches adolescence and fears pregnancy, resents the offender's efforts to control her or his life, dating, etc.
- The child encounters a caring adult he or she can trust and feels confident in disclosing to.
- The child has a urinary infection or other physical problem that causes him or her to seek medical care.

Appendix 6

Anatomical Doll Companies

Hyland Anatomical Dolls
4463 Torrance Blvd.
Torrance, CA 90503
(800) 333-4157 phone

Kids Rights
10100 Park Cedar Drive
Charlotte, NC 28210
(704) 541-0100 phone
(704) 541-0113 fax

Migima Designs
P.O. Box 5582
Eugene, OR 97405
(503) 343-3440 phone

(503) 683-3821 fax
(503) 228-5651 Portland office

Teach-A-Bodies
3509 Acorn Run
Ft. Worth, TX 76109
(817) 923-2380 phone
(817) 923-9774 fax

References

August, R. L., & Forman, B. D. (1989). A comparison of sexually abused and non-sexually abused children's behavioral responses to anatomically correct dolls. *Child Psychiatry and Human Development, 20(1)*, 39-47.

Bays, J. (1990). Are the genitalia of anatomical dolls distorted? *Child Abuse & Neglect, 14*, 171-175.

Boat, B. W., & Everson, M. D. (1986). *Using anatomical dolls: Guidelines for interviewing young children in sexual abuse investigations.* Chapel Hill: University of North Carolina, Department of Psychiatry.

Boat, B. W., & Everson, M. D. (1988a). Interviewing young children with anatomical dolls. *Child Welfare, 68(4)*, 337-352.

Boat, B. W., & Everson, M. D. (1988b). Use of anatomical dolls among professionals in sexual abuse evaluations. *Child Abuse & Neglect, 12*, 171-179.

Britton, H. L., & O'Keefe, M. A. (1991). Use of nonanatomical dolls in the sexual abuse interview. *Child Abuse & Neglect, 15*, 567-573.

Bulkey, J. (1985). Papers from a *National Policy Policy Conference on Legal Reforms in Child Sexual Abuse Cases.* (Available from American Bar Association, 1800 M Street N.W., Washington DC 20036).

Cohn, D. S. (1991). Anatomical doll play of preschoolers referred for sexual abuse and those not referred. *Child Abuse & Neglect, 15*, 455-466.

Dawson, B., & Geddie, L. (1991). *Low income, minority preschoolers' behavior with sexually anatomically detailed dolls.* Unpublished manuscript. (Available from Brenda Dawson, University of Montana, Department of Psychology, Missoula, MT)

Dawson, B., Vaughn, A. R., & Wagner, W. F. (1992). Normal responses to sexually anatomically detailed dolls. *Journal of Family Violence, 7(2)*, 135-152.

Dooley, S. (1985). *My day at the courthouse.* West Linn, OR: Trials and Smiles.

Everson, M. D., & Boat, B. W. (1990). Sexualized play among young children: Implications for the use of anatomical dolls in sexual abuse evaluation. *Journal of the American Academy of Child and Adolescent Psychiatry, 29,* 736-742.

Everson, M. D., Meyers, J.E.B., & White, S. (1993). *Proposed guidelines for use of anatomical dolls during investigations or evaluations of suspected child sexual abuse.* Unpublished manuscript. (Available from Program on Childhood Trauma and Maltreatment, Department of Psychiatry, University of North Carolina, Chapel Hill, NC 27599-7160)

Freeman, K. R., & Estrada-Mullaney, T. (1988). Using dolls to interview child victims: Legal concerns and interview procedures. *National Institute of Justice Reports, 207,* 2-6.

Friedemann [Edwards], V., & Morgan, M. (1985). *Interviewing sexual abuse victims using anatomical dolls: The professional's guidebook.* Eugene, OR: Migima Designs.

Gabriel, R. M. (1985). Anatomically correct dolls in the diagnosis of sexual abuse of children. *Journal of the Melanie Klein Society, 30,* 40-50.

Glaser, D., & Collins, C. (1989). The response of young, non-sexually abused children to anatomically correct dolls. *Journal of Child Psychology and Psychiatry, 30*(4), 547-560.

Goodman, G. S., & Aman, C. (1990). Children's use of anatomically detailed dolls to recount an event. *Child Development, 61,* 1859-1871.

Gwat-Yong, L., & Inman, A. (1991). The use of anatomical dolls as assessment and evidentiary tools. *Social Work, 36,* 396-399.

Hewitt, S. K., & Lund, S. J. (1988). *Evaluating the very young child for sexual abuse.* Unpublished manuscript. (Available from Midwest Children's Resource Center, Children's Hospital, St. Paul, MN)

Jampole, L., & Weber, M. K. (1987). An assessment of the behavior of sexually abused and nonsexually abused children with anatomically correct dolls. *Child Abuse & Neglect, 11,* 187-192.

Kendall-Tackett, K. A. (1992). Professionals' standards of "normal" behavior with anatomical dolls and factors that influence these standards. *Child Abuse & Neglect, 16,* 727-733.

Kendall-Tackett, K. A., & Watson, M. W. (1992). Use of anatomical dolls by Boston area professionals. *Child Abuse & Neglect, 16,* 423-428.

Leventhal, J. M., Hamilton, J., Rekedal, S., Tebano-Micci, A., & Eyster, C. (1989). Anatomically correct dolls used in interviews of young children suspected of having been sexually abused. *Pediatrics, 84*(5), 900-906.

Levy, J., Kalinowski, N., Markovic, J., Pittman, M., & Ahart, S. (1991). *Victim-sensitive interviewing in child sexual abuse: A developmental approach to interviewing and consideration of the use of anatomically correct dolls.* Chicago: Mount Sinai Hospital Medical Center, Department of Pediatrics.

MacFarlane, K., & Feldmeth, J. R. (Eds.) (1988). *RESPONSE child sexual abuse: The clinical interview.* New York: Guilford.

Philippus, M. J., & Koch, G. V. (1986). How to evaluate sexuality in children and to avoid using anatomically correct dolls. *Trial Talk,* 372-373.

Quinn, K. M., White, S., & Santilli, G. (1989). Influences of an interviewer's behavior in child sexual abuse investigations. *Bulletin of the American Academy of Psychiatry and Law, 17*(1), 45-52.

Realmuto, G. M., Jensen, J. B., & Wescoe, S. (1990). Specificity and sensitivity of sexually anatomically correct dolls in substantiating abuse: A pilot study. *Journal of the American Academy of Child and Adolescent Psychiatry, 29,* 743-746.

Saywitz, K. F., Goodman, G. S., Nicholas, E., & Moan, S. (1991). Children's memories of physical examinations involving genital touch: Implications for reports of child sexual abuse. *Journal of Consulting and Clinical Psychology, 59,* 682-691.

Shamroy, J. A. (1987, March/April). Interviewing the sexually abused child with anatomically correct dolls. *Social Work,* 165-166.

Sivan, A. B., Schor, D. P., Koeppl, G. K., & Noble, L. D. (1988). Interaction of normal children with anatomical dolls. *Child Abuse & Neglect, 12,* 295-304.

Walker, L.E.A. (1988). New techniques for assessment and evaluation of child sexual abuse victims: Using anatomically "correct" dolls and videotape procedures. In L.E.A. Walker (Ed.), *Handbook on sexual abuse of children* (pp. 175-197). New York: Springer.

White, S., Strom, G., Santilli, G., & Halpin, B. (1986). Interviewing young children with anatomically correct dolls. *Child Abuse & Neglect, 10,* 519-529.

White, S., Strom, G., Santilli, G., & Quinn, K. M. (1987a). *Clinical guidelines for interviewing young children with anatomically correct dolls.* Unpublished manuscript. (Available from Case Western Reserve University School of Medicine, Metro Health Center, 3395 Scranton Rd., Cleveland, OH 44109)

White, S., Strom, G., Santilli, G., & Quinn, K. M. (1987b). *Guidelines for interviewing pre-schoolers with sexually anatomically correct dolls.* Unpublished manuscript. (Available from Case Western Reserve University School of Medicine, Metro Health Center, 3395 Scranton Rd., Cleveland, OH 44109)

Yates, A., & Terr, L. (1988a). Debate forum: Anatomically correct dolls: Should they be used as the basis for expert testimony? *Journal of the American Academy of Child and Adolescent Psychiatry, 27,* 254-257.

Yates, A., & Terr, L. (1988b). Debate forum issue continued: Anatomically correct dolls: Should they be used as the basis for expert testimony? *Journal of the American Academy of Child and Adolescent Psychiatry, 27,* 387-388.

Bibliography

American Academy of Child and Adolescent Psychiatry. (1988). Guidelines for the clinical evaluation of child and adolescent sexual abuse. *Journal of the American Academy of Child and Adolescent Psychiatry, 27*, 655-657.

American Professional Society on the Abuse of Children. (1990). *Guidelines for psychosocial evaluation of suspected sexual abuse in young children.* Unpublished manuscript. (Available from American Professional Society on the Abuse of Children, 332 S. Michigan Ave., Suite 1600, Chicago, IL 60604)

American Psychological Association. (1991). *Statement on the use of anatomically detailed dolls in forensic evaluations.* Unpublished manuscript. (Available from American Psychological Association, 1200 17th Street., NW, Washington, DC 20036)

August, R. L., & Forman, B. D. (1989). A comparison of sexually abused and non-sexually abused children's behavioral responses to anatomically correct dolls. *Child Psychiatry and Human Development, 20(1),* 39-47.

Bays, J. (1990). Are the genitalia of anatomical dolls distorted? *Child Abuse & Neglect, 14,* 171-175.

Berliner, L. (1988). Anatomical dolls. *Journal of Interpersonal Violence, 3,* 468-470.

Boat, B. W., & Everson, M. D. (1986). *Using anatomical dolls: Guidelines for interviewing young children in sexual abuse investigations.* Chapel Hill: University of North Carolina, Department of Psychiatry.

Boat, B. W., & Everson, M. D. (1988a). Interviewing young children with anatomical dolls. *Child Welfare, 68(4),* 337-352.

Boat, B. W., & Everson, M. D. (1988b). Use of anatomical dolls among professionals in sexual abuse evaluations. *Child Abuse & Neglect, 12,* 171-179.

Boat, B. W., & Everson, M. D. (1993). The use of anatomical dolls in sexual abuse evaluations: Current research and practice. In G. Goodman & Bottoms (Eds.), *Child victims, child witnesses: Understanding and improving testimony* (pp. 47-70). New York: Guilford.

Boat, B. W., & Everson, M. D. (1994). Anatomical doll exploration among non-referred children: Comparisons by age, gender, race, and socioeconomic status. *Child Abuse & Neglect, 18*(4), 113-129.

Boat, B. W., Everson, M. D., & Holland, J. (1990). Maternal perceptions of nonabused young children's behavior after the children's exposure to anatomical dolls. *Child Welfare, 59*(5), 389-400.

Britton, H. L., & O'Keefe, M. A. (1991). Use of nonanatomical dolls in the sexual abuse interview. *Child Abuse & Neglect, 15*, 567-573.

Bulkley, J. (1985). Papers from a *National Policy Policy Conference on Legal Reforms in Child Sexual Abuse Cases.* (Available from American Bar Association, 1800 M Street N.W., Washington DC 20036).

Cohn, D. S. (1991). Anatomical doll play of preschoolers referred for sexual abuse and those not referred. *Child Abuse & Neglect, 15*, 455-466.

Conerly, S. (1986). Assessment of suspected child sexual abuse. In K. MacFarlane & J. Waterman (Eds.), *Sexual abuse of young children: Evaluation and treatment* (pp. 30-51). New York: Guilford.

Conte, J. R., Sorenson, E., Fogarty, L., & Rosa, J. (1991). Evaluating children's reports of sexual abuse: Results from a survey of professionals. *American Journal of Orthopsychiatry, 61*, 428-437.

Dawson, B., & Geddie, L. (1991). *Low income, minority preschoolers' behavior with sexually anatomically detailed dolls.* Unpublished manuscript. (Available from Brenda Dawson, University of Montana, Department of Psychology, Missoula, MT)

Dawson, B., Vaughn, A. R., & Wagner, W. F. (1992). Normal responses to sexually anatomically detailed dolls. *Journal of Family Violence, 7*(2), 135-152.

Dooley, S. (1985). *My day at the courthouse.* West Linn, OR: Trials and Smiles.

Everson, M. D., & Boat, B. W. (1989). False allegations of sexual abuse by children and adolescents. *Journal of the American Academy of Child and Adolescent Psychiatry, 28*, 230-235.

Everson, M. D., & Boat, B. W. (1990). Sexualized play among young children: Implications for the use of anatomical dolls in sexual abuse evaluation. *Journal of the American Academy of Child and Adolescent Psychiatry, 29*, 736-742.

Everson, M. D., Meyers, J.E.B., & White, S. (1993). *Proposed guidelines for use of anatomical dolls during investigations or evaluations of suspected child sexual abuse.* Unpublished manuscript. (Available from Program on Childhood Trauma and Maltreatment, Department of Psychiatry, University of North Carolina, Chapel Hill, NC 27599-7160)

Faller, K. L. (1988). Criteria for judging the credibility of children's statements about their sexual abuse. *Child Welfare, 67*(5), 389-401.

Freeman, K. R., & Estrada-Mullaney, T. (1988). Using dolls to interview child victims: Legal concerns and interview procedures. *National Institute of Justice Reports, 207*, 2-6.

Friedemann [Edwards], V., & Morgan, M. (1985). *Interviewing sexual abuse victims using anatomical dolls: The professional's guidebook.* Eugene, OR: Migima Designs.

Gabriel, R. M. (1985). Anatomically correct dolls in the diagnosis of sexual abuse of children. *Journal of the Melanie Klein Society, 30*, 40-50.

Glaser, D., & Collins, C. (1989). The response of young, non-sexually abused children to anatomically correct dolls. *Journal of Child Psychology and Psychiatry, 30*(4), 547-560.

Goodman, G. S., & Aman, C. (1990). Children's use of anatomically detailed dolls to recount an event. *Child Development, 61*, 1859-1871.

Gwat-Yong, L., & Inman, A. (1991). The use of anatomical dolls as assessment and evidentiary tools. *Social Work, 36*, 396-399.

Harnest, J. (1988). *An effective resource for sex education, investigation, therapy, and courtroom testimony.* Fort Worth, TX: Teach-A-Bodies.

Harnest, J., & Chavern, H. (1985). *A survey of the use of anatomically correct dolls in sex education investigation, therapy and courtroom testimony.* Paper presented at the 7th World Congress of Sociology, New Delhi, India.

Hewitt, S. K., & Lund, S. J. (1988). *Evaluating the very young child for sexual abuse.* Unpublished manuscript. (Available from Midwest Children's Resource Center, Children's Hospital, St. Paul, MN)

Hindman, J. (1987). *Step-by-step: Sixteen steps toward legally sound sexual abuse investigations.* Ontario, OR: Alexandria Associates.

Jampole, L., & Weber, M. K. (1987). An assessment of the behavior of sexually abused and nonsexually abused children with anatomically correct dolls. *Child Abuse & Neglect, 11*, 187-192.

Jones, D.P.H. (1992). *Interviewing the sexually abused child.* London: Gaskell.

Jones, D.P.H., & McGraw, J. M. (1987). Reliable and fictitious accounts of sexual abuse of children. *Journal of Interpersonal Violence, 2*, 27-45.

Jones, D.P.H., & McQuiston, M. (1986). *Interviewing the sexually abused child.* Denver: Henry Kempe National Center for the Prevention and Treatment of Child Abuse and Neglect.

Kendall-Tackett, K. A. (1992). Professionals' standards of "normal" behavior with anatomical dolls and factors that influence these standards. *Child Abuse & Neglect, 16*, 727-733.

Kendall-Tackett, K. A., & Watson, M. W. (1992). Use of anatomical dolls by Boston area professionals. *Child Abuse & Neglect, 16*, 423-428.

Leventhal, J. M., Hamilton, J., Rekedal, S., Tebano-Micci, A., & Eyster, C. (1989). Anatomically correct dolls used in interviews of young children suspected of having been sexually abused. *Pediatrics, 84*(5), 900-906.

Levy, J., Kalinowski, N., Markovic, J., Pittman, M., & Ahart, S. (1991). *Victim-sensitive interviewing in child sexual abuse: A developmental approach to interviewing and consideration of the use of anatomically correct dolls.* Chicago: Mount Sinai Hospital Medical Center, Department of Pediatrics.

MacFarlane, K., & Feldmeth, J. R. (Eds.). (1988). *RESPONSE child sexual abuse: The clinical interview.* New York: Guilford.

MacFarlane, K., & Krebs, S. (1986). Techniques for interviewing and evidence gathering. In K. MacFarlane & J. Waterman (Eds.), *Sexual abuse of young children: Evaluation and treatment* (pp. 67-100). New York: Guilford.

Mann, C. (1991). Assessment of sexually abused children with anatomically detailed dolls: A critical review. *Behavioral Sciences and the Law, 9*, 43-51.

McIver, W., Wakefield, H., & Ungerwager, R. (1987). *Behavior of abused and nonabused children in interviews with anatomically correct dolls.* Unpublished manuscript. (Available from Institute for Psychological Therapy, 13200 Canyon City Blvd., Northfield, MN 55057)

Naumann, R. (1985). *The case of the indecent dolls or can voodoo be professional?* Unpublished manuscript. (Available from Department of Educational Psychology, Northern Illinois University, DeKalb, IL 60115-2853)

Philippus, M. J., & Koch, G. V. (1986). How to evaluate sexuality in children and to avoid using anatomically correct dolls. *Trial Talk, 372-373.*

Quinn, K. M., White, S., & Santilli, G. (1989). Influences of an interviewer's behavior in child sexual abuse investigations. *Bulletin of the American Academy of Psychiatry and Law, 17*(1), 45-52.

Realmuto, G. M., Jensen, J. B., & Wescoe, S. (1990). Specificity and sensitivity of sexually anatomically correct dolls in substantiating abuse: A pilot study. *Journal of the American Academy of Child and Adolescent Psychiatry, 29,* 743-746.

Saywitz, K. F., Goodman, G. S., Nicholas, E., & Moan, S. (1991). Children's memories of physical examinations involving genital touch: Implications for reports of child sexual abuse. *Journal of Consulting and Clinical Psychology, 59,* 682-691.

Sgroi, S. M. (1984). *Guidelines for using anatomically correct dolls for investigation of child sexual abuse.* Unpublished manuscript. (Available from Mt. Sinai Hospital, 500 Blue Hills Ave., Hartford, CT 06112)

Shamroy, J. A. (1987, March/April). Interviewing the sexually abused child with anatomically correct dolls. *Social Work,* 165-166.

Sivan, A. B., Schor, D. P., Koeppl, G. K., & Noble, L. D. (1988). Interaction of normal children with anatomical dolls. *Child Abuse & Neglect, 12,* 295-304.

Skinner, L. J., & Berry, K. K. (1993). Anatomically detailed dolls and the evaluations of child sexual abuse allegations. *Law and Human Behavior, 17,* 399-421.

Spaulding, W. (1987). *Interviewing child victims of sexual exploitation.* Washington, DC: National Center for Missing and Exploited Children.

Steward, M. S., Bussey, K., Goodman, G. S., & Saywitz, K. J. (1993). Implications of developmental research for interviewing children. *Child Abuse & Neglect, 17*(1), 25-37.

Swan, A. B., Schor, D. P., Koeppl, G. K., & Noble, L. D. (1988). Interaction of normal children with anatomical dolls. *Child Abuse & Neglect, 12,* 295-304.

Vaughn, A. R., Dawson, B., & Wagner, W. G. (1989). *The use of anatomically detailed dolls in the investigation of child sexual abuse.* Paper presented at Association for Advancement of Behavior Therapy, Washington, DC.

Walker, L.E.A. (1988). New techniques for assessment and evaluation of child sexual abuse victims: Using anatomically "correct" dolls and videotape procedures. In L.E.A. Walker (Ed.), *Handbook on sexual abuse of children* (pp. 175-197). New York: Springer.

Wescott, H., Davis, G., & Clifford, B. (1989). The use of anatomical dolls in child witness interviews. *Adoption and Fostering, 13,* 6-14.

White, S. (1986). Uses and abuses of the sexually anatomically correct dolls. *Division of Child, Youth and Family Services Newsletter* (APA Division 37), *9,* 3-6.

White, S. (1988). Should investigatory use of anatomical dolls be defined by the courts? *Journal of Interpersonal Violence, 3,* 471-475.

White, S., & Santilli, G. (1988). A review of clinical practices and research data on anatomical dolls. *Journal of Interpersonal Violence, 3,* 430-442.

White, S., Strom, G. S., & Santilli, G. (1985). *Interviewing young sexual abuse victims with anatomically correct dolls.* Unpublished manuscript. (Available from Cleveland Metropolitan General Hospital, Metro Health Center, 3395 Scranton Rd., Cleveland, OH 44109)

White, S., Strom, G., Santilli, G., & Halpin, B. (1986). Interviewing young children with anatomically correct dolls. *Child Abuse & Neglect, 10,* 519-529.

White, S., Strom, G., Santilli, G., & Quinn, K. M. (1987a). *Clinical guidelines for interviewing young children with anatomically correct dolls.* Unpublished manuscript. (Available from Case Western Reserve University School of Medicine, Metro Health Center, 3395 Scranton Rd., Cleveland, OH 44109)

White, S., Strom, G., Santilli, G., & Quinn, K. M. (1987b). *Guidelines for interviewing pre-schoolers with sexually anatomically correct dolls.* Unpublished manuscript. (Available from Case Western Reserve University School of Medicine, Metro Health Center, 3395 Scranton Rd., Cleveland, OH 44109)

Yates, A., & Terr, L. (1988a). Debate forum: Anatomically correct dolls: Should they be used as the basis for expert testimony? *Journal of the American Academy of Child and Adolescent Psychiatry, 27,* 254-257.

Yates, A., & Terr, L. (1988b). Debate forum issue continued: Anatomically correct dolls: Should they be used as the basis for expert testimony? *Journal of the American Academy of Child and Adolescent Psychiatry, 27,* 387-388.

Index

About the Author

Marcia Morgan, Ph.D., is an author, consultant, researcher, and lecturer on sexual assault prevention and investigation. She lectures internationally to police, schools, and professional conferences on rape, sexual harassment, and sexual abuse of children. She was a deputy sheriff/crime prevention officer for 7 years, research associate on a 3-year National Institute of Mental Health grant evaluating rape prevention and resistance strategies, and for several years a lobbyist in Oregon and Washington, DC. She is the author of two books on sexual abuse, *Safe Touch* and *My Feelings,* and two videos on children's safety, *It's OK to Say No* and *Aware and Not Afraid.*

Marcia Morgan and Virginia Edwards were the original developers of the anatomical dolls in 1976. The dolls are now used worldwide in child sexual abuse cases. They pioneered work in this field and coauthored the book *Interviewing Sexual Abuse Victims Using Anatomical Dolls: The Professional's Guidebook* (1985).

About the
Contributing Author

Virginia Edwards, B.A., has worked for the State of Oregon since 1980. As a caseworker for Children's Services Division, she worked in protective services, permanency planning, and family sex abuse treatment services. As a casework supervisor, she has supervised substitute care caseloads, permanent planning caseloads, family sex abuse treatment, family treatment, parent training, and adoptions. Before working for CSD, she worked as a patrol officer and detective for a municipal police department specializing in sexual assault investigations. She offers workshops on interviewing children and case planning/case management for sexual abuse/sibling incest cases. She is a graduate of Oregon State University.

Morgan and Edwards are available for professional training seminars and can be reached through Migima Designs, P.O. Box 5582, Eugene, OR 97405.